To Dorothy,
- good friend and
Keeper of wisdom
Love, Pat
July 9/12

SURPRISED PINK GERANIUMS

a memoir

PAT BROWN

iUniverse, Inc.
Bloomington

Surprised Pink Geraniums
A Memior

iUniverse books may be ordered through booksellers or by contacting:

iUniverse
1663 Liberty Drive
Bloomington, IN 47403
www.iuniverse.com
1-800-Authors (1-800-288-4677)

*Because of the dynamic nature of the Internet, any web addresses or links contained in this
book may have changed since publication and may no longer be valid. The views expressed
in this work are solely those of the author and do not necessarily reflect the views of the
publisher, and the publisher hereby disclaims any responsibility for them.*

*Any people depicted in stock imagery provided by Thinkstock are models,
and such images are being used for illustrative purposes only.*

Certain stock imagery © Thinkstock.

ISBN: 978-1-4697-9080-0 (sc)
ISBN: 978-1-4697-9078-7 (e)
ISBN: 978-1-4697-9079-4 (dj)

Library of Congress Control Number: 2012904490

Printed in the United States of America

iUniverse rev. date: 4/13/2012

cover art by Nancy Kursbatt

author photo by John Pender

for Tom

contents

Part Five Grief and God

Part Six Disruptions, Epiphanies and Peace…(repeat)

Prologue

Slippery black earth
Surprised pink geraniums
Terra-cotta shards.

By eleven o'clock a tropical air mass had dropped over the city of Toronto like a hot, wet cocoon. It deadened the senses and sucked the life out of any initiative beyond eye blinking. The oppressive heat had been hanging around all week.

As Tom and I rushed about making last minute preparations, I wished we had given more consideration to an October or even a Christmas wedding. June's unpredictable weather was something I couldn't control, so I had decided not to worry about it, until now, just hours before the ceremony.

Planning this wedding ceremony had been joyous. Choosing the music and then making the tapes had given me hours of focused happiness. I had sat cross-legged on the floor with piles of audio tapes surrounding me like a kid with boxes and boxes of new Lego to play with. Tom had left most of the music decisions to me. I was a mixer in a studio doing work that was tedious, stressful and enormously satisfying. The highlight would be Handel's "Hallelujah Chorus" blasting from hidden speakers the moment after the vows were exchanged. Later, over dinner and dancing, Tom's favourites from Willie Nelson and Kris Kristofferson would be played.

The wedding was to be outdoors. Our good friends Derek and Judy had generously donated their lovely back yard on Eighth Street, just a few doors away from where I had lived for many years. Their garden was shaded by a leafy canopy of trees, and hundreds of flowers bloomed everywhere in pots and in beds.

Weeks before, Tom and I had enjoyed choosing the menu and the wines for the dinner. Having a dress made that would look reasonably bridal but also do service afterwards had been fun. In fact, the planning was so much more enjoyable (and peaceful) than it had been the first time around. That wedding was a tribal ritual orchestrated by my mother, the aunts, and the church. This time, my mother was an honoured guest, the aunts couldn't come, and the church wasn't invited. This wedding would be a joyous celebration of life and love and laughter and friendship.

Now that the day had come, even the oppressive weather couldn't affect my mood. I had a leisurely breakfast with my mother and my daughter Jennifer. My hair was styled, nails brought to attention and face sculpted to as close to bridal beauty as it would ever be. I had fled when the beautician suggested further tweaking of the face and body. I wanted to be recognizable; I didn't want Tom peering at me during the wedding to make sure I was the woman he had offered to share his dental plan with.

The rest of the morning was spent on hurried phone calls, checking with Judy that chairs, tables, wine and food were either delivered or on the way. The caterer assured me that all was well; the food was indeed being prepared and packed as we spoke, and yes, the waitstaff would be there at the appointed time.

I was also keeping an eye on the great dark clouds banking to the west and north of us. My bargaining with the weather gods had suggested a short break (just long enough for a wedding) before the deluge.

Months ago I had decided to provide the pots of flowers and greenery that would flank the patio where the ceremony would be performed. The geraniums were in full bloom and radiantly pink. Tom and I had brought the flowers down to Eighth Street the day before, but one last pot couldn't be crammed into the car. Tom had promised to bring it down the next day.

By noon I was feeling almost feverish with the heat and the constant litany that kept chanting in my head; all the *what ifs* and *did I remembers* had become exhausting. But by two o'clock only one chore remained, to pick up my almost-forgotten wedding dress at the apartment where Tom and I had lived for almost a year.

When I stepped off the elevator on the eleventh floor that sultry afternoon in June, I looked up and saw Tom hurrying towards me and the open doors of the elevator. His arms were wrapped around an enormous pot of pink geraniums. He saw me and stumbled. In slow motion, the pot of geraniums fell to the floor. Terra-cotta shards, crumbling black earth, petals and leaves littered the tile floor, but the pink geraniums were still intact—looking surprised but still happy.

Minutes later everything would be scooped up with most of the lovely black earth and carefully mounded into a new pot. But before that, just before everything hit the ground, Tom and I had leaned toward each other, trying to catch the falling pot. We missed, but our eyes caught and held. We stared at each other, as shocked as the geraniums.

As Tom's hands lost their grip on the flowers, his face took on that look of horror when something awful, something inevitable, is about to happen. But when he raised his eyes, a small crevice in time winked open, and nothing existed except an unbounded joy. An awareness that a moment can contain the world. A marriage happened in that moment, and our witness was a pot of geraniums.

A few hours later, the powerful and sacred words that we repeated in front of human witnesses remembered and honoured an event already in the past—and perhaps the future. Because in that future a moment would come when that "crevice in time", and the memory of its grace, was able to pull me back from despair.

Later that day, remarkably, the weather gods paid attention. My first husband was a meteorologist. He undoubtedly would have a sane and scientific explanation for the change in weather. But my understanding of the change was based on a more inclusive view of the universe. One where a desperate bride can influence the course of events, if only as a very small meteorological shift. One where two women blowing into the wind might influence the course of an amiable cloud. This is how it happened.

Many weeks before the wedding, Tom and I had stood on our balcony admiring a lovely sunset. In a moment of laughter, he showed me how, by focusing our minds, we could move the clouds around and create a small opening for sunshine and light to pass through. With a great deal of scepticism, I did as I was told, and surprisingly, the clouds shifted. Even though I insisted that it was sheer coincidence and clouds shifted all the time, the moment stayed with me.

On the day of the wedding, just before leaving for Eighth Street, I stood with Judy, my matron of honour, on the balcony looking at the dark, billowing clouds massing in the northwestern sky. Tom had said that if you stare at a cloud, focus your attention, imagine it slowly shifting direction and then gently blow, the clouds will move. As I explained this to her, Judy looked at me with alarm, obviously having serious doubts about my sanity. "Try it," I said. "You know Tom is never wrong about these things."

So we did. Two middle aged women in their wedding finery feeling not a bit ridiculous, leaned out over a balcony railing. We focused on the massing clouds that were getting closer and darker by the minute. We stared at those clouds and blew at them until there was no breath left to blow. And then we watched, in awe, as the clouds slowly shifted direction. An opening of the purest blue appeared in the western sky and extended itself southward.

We left quickly in case the universe decided to stop being accommodating. By the time we arrived on Eighth St., all of southern Toronto was bathed in light streaming through the last of the drifting clouds. A wild wind, fresh and clean, was blowing steadily.

Much later when it was all over, after two squad cars from Twenty-One Division with screaming sirens had escorted us all the way home, we lay in bed smiling in the dark. I turned to Tom and said, "Judy and I blew the clouds away, you know."

"I thought you might have done," he said, and then my bridegroom fell asleep.

A few days later we left on a two-week honeymoon cruise on a Greek ship somewhat past her prime but not quite seedy. It took us from Venice to Greece, the Greek islands, Egypt, Turkey and Israel. We flew into Venice and tried to see as much as we could of this magical city while being hustled through streets dripping with history and a bit of romantic menace. As honeymoons go, it was magical, mystical, exhausting and full of laughter.

Tom and I travelled to many places over the years. Always wanting to explore the unfamiliar, whether it was hiking into the jungle in Venezuela, or, in the midst of a never-ending Canadian winter, we would fly anywhere that didn't require snowboots. But the adventure that started on the day Tom dropped the pot of pink geraniums has never ended. Just changed.

Part One
Before the Beginning

Eighth Street stories

Before Tom Brown entered my life, I lived in a south Toronto neighbourhood that was part of the catchment area for Metropolitan Toronto's Twenty-One Division. The very place where Tom worked as a police community relations officer. And yet, I managed to live in that quiet, leafy neighbourhood for seven years before our paths crossed. The stories that follow are stories of places and people. Before my life changed. Before the geraniums.

finding Eighth Street

In the summer of 1980 when I was thirty-eight, five years divorced and in the middle of a life, I bought a small brick house in an almost-forgotten pocket of southwestern Toronto called New Toronto. It had no great sports or entertainment complexes, little industry and its Lake Ontario beaches were so tucked away only the closest neighbourhoods knew about them.

The small local movie theatre (which closed in the mid-eighties) showed third-run movies but you could walk there on a Sunday afternoon, put your feet up if you were careful, eat popcorn, smoke if you were still addicted and greet your neighbours. Most of our teenaged daughters took their turn selling popcorn and taking tickets for little money but a chance to feel important and watch free movies.

My daughter Jennifer was a "popcorn girl" for a while but that was only after she stopped being unhappy about our move. She turned sixteen in 1980 and was deeply embedded in our former neighbourhood a few miles north. She was particularly unhappy about having to change high schools. She soon discovered, to her amazement, that Mimico High, in spite of being classed as more "downscale" than Royal York, had good teachers and less weed.

John, my fifteen-year-old son was supremely uninterested in school regardless of its place on the social scale. He had many far more important irons in the fire. Trying to look like a reincarnation of Jimmy Dean was one of them. His citizen's band radio was another.

The year before our move, I had gone back to school myself to get a graduate degree at the University of Toronto. One of my first tasks was to turn the sunny front porch into a peaceful place to read and write and dream. Sitting out there I could feel the stillness of my new neighbourhood settle around me.

The house was half a block south of Lakeshore Boulevard and two blocks north of Lake Ontario. Because of the flatness of the neighbourhood's streets and the limited amount of traffic, the area was great for bicycling or walking. The edge of the lake where Fifth Street ended had a pumping and water filtration station with an acre or so of grass surrounding it. A perfect spot for a dog park, and so it came to be.

The municipal pool on Eleventh Street was a short walk in the other direction. "Adults only" swimming happened every noon-hour and that was where my handsome mailman made a gentlemanly pass and where, another day, a small child shat in the shallow end. After a thorough disinfection, we were all back two days later, including the mailman, who never made another pass but smiled sweetly when he delivered the mail. I had a small pang at turning aside his interest. He was young and handsome (maybe too young and handsome) but more importantly, he wasn't what was missing in my life.

I didn't know I was looking, but I knew that if I were, he wasn't the answer. There were other men who drifted into my life during those Eighth Street years, but they soon drifted out again, leaving my heart aching but not broken.

Ben

Lakeshore Boulevard was the main street for shopping, for street cars, regular cars, old ladies and bicycles. It was where my son John saw a man beating a large yellow puppy before tying him up to a lamp post. When the man went into the nearby pub, leaving the dog cowering on the sidewalk, John untied him and brought him home. Of course I didn't hear that story until years later. What I heard when I got home from work that day was that a dog had followed John home and wouldn't leave. He had no tags and judging by the scars on his nose, he had been beaten. "So Mum, can he please, please stay?"

I looked into the dog's large, soft brown eyes and then into John's blue ones that still held traces of tears, and said, "What shall we call him?" And so, Ben came to stay. He was a cross between a Great Dane and an accommodating yellow Labrador. He and his special friend Georgette, a Samoyed/Husky cross, played endless games of who could run faster and jump higher in the dog park. Ben brought a great deal of joy into our lives after we got past those early weeks of "puppy training 101".

Although he became well-socialized, he maintained a dollop of suspicion. The old woman dressed in a long black coat and an enveloping kerchief regardless of the temperature as she pulled her squeaky-wheeled shopping cart, would set off a round of fierce barking. She kept to the middle of the road but never broke her stride. Ben, safe behind the screen door, was proud that he had done his job and scared her away. He was also pleased when the mailman left immediately after pushing his offerings through the mail slot. Only once did Ben show his rage at this intrusion by shredding an envelope. Unfortunately, it was one containing a cheque.

He was a brave dog but his bravery cost him moments of fear and trembling. One night, as my daughter Jennifer was taking Ben on his late evening walk, a rowdy group of men exited from the Lakeshore Lounge—a disreputable bar located a few blocks away. One of the men made a comment to his companions, leered at Jennifer, stumbled over to her, and put his arm around her. Jen was nervous: it was dark, it was late and she was seventeen. She pulled Ben closer and warned the man that she would set the dog loose. But the man only laughed and tightened his hold. Ben, who had been sitting quietly and politely by Jen's side, suddenly, leapt at the man and sank his teeth into his arm. Luckily, he was wearing a heavy jacket. But the shock and fear of 150 pounds of snarling dog was enough to send him on his way.

Meanwhile, Ben was quivering and trying to hide between Jen's legs. She had to soothe his fears, giving him lots of hugs and endearments before they could walk home. A "cowardly lion" indeed.

Ben's friend Georgette lived with my friends Derek and Judy just up the street. The humans would talk and walk as the dogs sniffed and played. Sometimes after work, Derek would drive Georgette down to the lake in his MG convertible. One day, when I was already there with Ben, he suggested that we all drive home in the MG. Both dogs were perched in the back of this tiny sports car, tongues lolling and looking happy. The tires squealed as Derek cornered too quickly onto Eighth Street. The dogs and I tried to hang on by our finger and toenails. I made it around the corner but they didn't. I looked back in horror to see two dogs tumbling onto the pavement. Luckily, the car was built close to the ground and even with Derek's cornering habits, we had not been going fast enough to cause any harm. Georgette hopped back into the car, but Ben sat down and looked at me, wondering if I was crazy enough to make him get back into the car. The decision was easy; the two of us continued home on foot even though our legs were now a little shaky. As Derek and Georgette sped by with a wave and a holler, Ben and I were thinking ahead to dinner as the curtains of Eighth Street dropped back into place.

That was Ben's last trip in Derek's MG. From then on, he wisely planted his very substantial feet on solid ground and looked in the other direction whenever he was invited for a ride. I didn't blame him and often felt like planting my own feet at the same suggestion.

more Eighth Street

One of my favourite pastimes on a Saturday morning in New Toronto was to go "Lakeshoring" with Ben and Jennifer. John, being a teenage boy, was either sleeping or out and about doing things that didn't include shopping or mothers. Our four cats, who had much the same diurnal rhythms as vampires (and perhaps teenage boys) would be asleep in whatever pools of sunshine or warmth that they could find.

So Ben, Jennifer and I would walk slowly along Lakeshore Boulevard, gaze into windows, pick up delicatessen food for lunch then stop at the bakery for a loaf of fresh, crusty bread, and maybe some cinnamon buns. We might check to see if Frank's Fashions window display had changed; not likely, since the same dusty fashions had been on display for several years.

As always, we would stop to admire the little shop with the big sign declaring, "Big Gods and Little Gods Sold Here". Lined up in the display window were statues of every deity, saint and icon that one could imagine. A fat smiling Buddha sat comfortably beside Jesus, while Kali and Ganesh seemed to be deep in conversation with Saint Teresa and a few other, unidentified friends.

When I first moved into this unique neighbourhood, there was talk of it soon becoming a new Cabbagetown, or even the new "Beach"— each of these neighbourhoods being the essence of trendy and therefore, expensive. So a certain amount of exterior painting and yard tidying in the neighbourhood was accomplished for the benefit of future mouthwatering profits. But it never came to pass. New Toronto stayed quietly off of the beaten path and the new paint soon began to lose its shine.

One lovely spring afternoon on Eighth Street while I was working on a term paper due the next day, I lifted my head when I heard sounds of excitement on my normally sleepy street. Mine was a neighbourhood where the trees shaded and protected their surroundings from too much sunlight or from other harsh realities of life. It was a quiet, non-gossipy kind of street. Several of its inhabitants were British war brides brought to Canada and eventually Eighth Street by their soldier husbands. They lived in well-constructed houses built for soldiers and their families after World War One. By 1980, these women had reached an advanced age. Many had died or were spending their last days in "homes" other than their own, but a few still remained.

Marjorie for example, my next-door neighbour, would walk by every morning just after the stores opened on Lakeshore Boulevard. I always enjoyed watching her since she had a forty-five degree tilt when she walked—as though she were headed into a gale-force wind and had to angle her body in order to make headway. There was never any weather to account for this peculiar way of walking; no doubt there was logic for it, but no one remembered what it was.

On this day, as I lifted my head at an unexpected noise, I couldn't believe what I saw framed by the porch window. Three chickens were clucking and strutting their way down the middle of the street. Behind them, tails up, bodies in stalking mode, crept two cats. Their little feline faces were full of joyful, focused intent. Birds they knew about. They were quite keen on birds much to the chagrin of the ancient war brides. But these were very large birds. Obviously caution was called for and caution is a large part of a cat's nature. But still, this could be a cat Christmas, Easter and Thanksgiving all rolled into one.

Behind these cautiously excited, stalking cats were three of the spryest of the street's war brides. It was their flapping and shooing noises that had awakened me from my musings at the typewriter.

Three old women were trying to chase those "evil" cats away from the chickens.

As I opened the front door for a better look, Ben decided that this was a spectacle much too interesting to ignore. So before I could stop him, he was away; out the door, down the walkway and into the street, joining the parade right behind the old ladies.

They mistook his gaping grin for danger and hurried even faster after the cats who in turn picked up the pace after the chickens. Ben was in his element. The old ladies were on a mission. The cats were hedging their bets as cats will do. For a few minutes the silent arching trees and the somnolent street was alive in a way it hadn't been for years.

Eventually, the chickens were rescued by their owners and the cats had stalked off wearing their disappointment with cat dignity. Ben had come rushing home, tongue lolling, and the large grin still on his face. We sat on the front steps together munching cookies.

Marjorie stopped by to share a cookie and pat Ben distractedly. "I hope those chickens are all right," she said in her soft Geordie accent worn down by sixty years in Canada. We agreed that it had been an exciting afternoon for Eighth Street. Marjorie then set her course with sails trimmed and home port in sight.

deliverance

Before Tom, when I was divorced, single and sometimes lonely, my friends Derek and Judy would occasionally drag me along on their trips into the world beyond Eighth Street. Even though they had found each other late in life and were very much in love, they rarely simpered at each other and I never felt like a third wheel.

Most of our outings involved concerts or plays or trips to a nearby Indian restaurant that was run by a pair of Cockneys who served good British beer and excellent curry. One summer, during a particularly hot and humid week, they invited me to go on a camping trip. Camping was one of their favourite things for a summer weekend, but I was a city girl. Cottages were fine if they had all or at least most of the amenities, but I always felt that certain personal activities were best done in the comfort of a well-appointed bathroom, bedroom or kitchen. I consulted Ben about the camping trip. He just wagged his tail feverishly and drooled at the prospect of a whole weekend with Georgette, not only the love of his life but his canine co-protector of Eighth Street. Since my two teenagers were to be away for the week end and my social life was pretty skimpy that summer, camping it would be.

Friday afternoon at a campsite by the Credit, a quiet unassuming river an hour or so northwest of Toronto, my novice status became obvious as I watched Judy unpack her "kitchen". She did not believe in roughing it when it came to food. The usual camping fare of burgers and hot dogs were never on the menu. As she worked, she wisely turned down my offers to help by saying that she had a ritual and she needed to know exactly where everything was. The tents were also pitched quickly and without my help. I tried to make myself useful but ended up scrambling just to get out of the way. I was in awe of their competence but tired of feeling useless and clumsy. I wandered off to sit by the river with the dogs and a book; a novel about a bunch of men on a camping trip who get into a bit of trouble with some local rednecks.

Later we swam and tubed down the river and drank just enough wine to enhance our appetite for dinner. We dined on lamb chops, garlic mashed potatoes, frenched green beans with buttery slivered almonds and a green salad. I helped with clean-up and other chores that didn't require great skill. Later, Ben and I settled down for a surprisingly peaceful night's sleep. Surprising, because I expected a sleeping bag and a thin air mattress to be impediments to comfort. Not to mention the possibility of strange or even frightening creatures stalking and perhaps eating each other within earshot. But sleep came quickly and neither Ben nor I moved until morning—early morning.

Before breakfast, even before coffee, I was amazed to see that Judy and Derek were pulling on hiking boots. And it is hard to be amazed while still only half-awake.

"Come on, Pat, it's a beautiful day. A hike before breakfast is on the agenda."

I decided that a weak smile would be the best if not the most honest response. So away we went. Ben and Georgette galumphed ahead on a trail that wound away from the river, through the trees, up hills and through sunny clearings. The river raced over stones and fallen logs; if not always in sight, always within earshot.

Eventually, Ben began to tire. So did I. The pace had been not-quite, quick march but too fast for slackers. As the trail took another turn, I saw another hill and I stopped in my tracks. For the first time, I looked around with full attention. The sun was backlighting the birches and maples and glinting off the white water of the river below. On the other side of the trail, a small gulley was home to a curious family of racoons. I could hear birdsong and the chatter of squirrels.

When Ben saw that I had stopped, he left his still-bounding friend Georgette and came panting back to my side, tail wagging expectantly. "No more hiking Ben," I said to him, as I sat down on a grassy slope. I called to Derek and Judy who were almost out of sight, telling them I would see them back at the campsite. They barely broke stride but waved an acknowledgment.

For the next half-hour or so, Ben and I explored the woods, smelled the musty, earthy smell of last year's fallen leaves, and later, sat on a log by the side of the river. I took off my shoes, waded into the deliciously cool water, skipped a few stones, and then just lay on the bank inhaling and absorbing the world. Ben sat beside me and we became part of the stillness—not silence, there were too many songbirds and a river with much to say.

The hikers got back to camp moments after Ben and I. Soon Judy had whipped up pancakes filled with the fresh raspberries picked just after their hike. Both of them looked healthy and happy and energized. I suddenly realized that I loved them for their energy, their competence and their cheerful generosity. I also knew that I was happy and pleased with myself as well. I didn't feel the inadequacy of my left-footedness. I didn't feel lazy or incompetent at being on a camping trip in the middle of nowhere. And I didn't feel resentment because my friends had a different way of enjoying nature.

Feeling their warmth and friendship and their acceptance as we drank coffee beside the river, I realized they didn't care that my idea of going into the woods was very different from theirs. They drank in their surroundings through the soles of their hiking shoes. I drank it in while learning about active sitting. And as that awareness sank deep into my bones, the unease, the sense of not being good enough, was ridiculously easy to release. I was absorbed by that moment of profound peace: sipping coffee, scribbling in a notebook, watching Ben and Georgette chase each other in the sunshine and absorbing the closeness of my friends. Even though they were already making plans for another more challenging hike (*sans moi*).

That peaceful moment by the Credit River came in the midst of hectic and chaos-filled years of change and adaptation. After twelve years of marriage, divorce, and the raising of two children into stormy adolescence, I had finally started to grow into myself. To find those islands of peace which helped me to re-define the world. To discover the lovely paradox that there is always a place at the table for outsiders—as long as you choose the right table.

A wise adage says you must be at peace with yourself before you find love. Tom and I crossed paths soon after that camping trip. And life changed again.

Part Two
The Beginning

HIS NAME WAS TOM BROWN, no middle initial. He was born in the north east of England in a small coal mining town, and spent the years from his fifteenth birthday until he was twenty-four-years-old in the pit, hacking at the coal face. When he couldn't bear life as a mole any longer, he packed two suitcases and sailed to Canada. He spent time in construction jobs, getting a bonus if he was the only worker who spoke English. Later he joined the army, and eventually the Metropolitan Toronto Police Force.

He liked to think that, like his name, he was a simple man. He liked country and western music and people who wore cowboy hats—even though he would never wear one himself. In fact, if we were out shopping and he wanted to give me a giggle, we would head to the hat department. Tom would try on hats until I almost fell down with laughter. He liked cop shows on television and Clint Eastwood movies. He liked reviving cups of tea several times a day, Fig Newton cookies and fish and chips for dinner. He liked the Newcastle United soccer team but never developed a taste for hockey. He liked Louis L'Amour westerns and 87th Precinct detective stories. He liked being a cop so he could put bad guys away, help old ladies and lost children. He liked boats, dogs and, most of the time, he liked me.

Tom also liked watching tennis and ice dancing on television. He liked classical music and silence. He liked to grow spaces in his life He liked drumming and learning about native spirituality. He liked Tai Chi (and the women who taught him). He liked Kris Kristofferson even though Tom wasn't always sure about his politics—with age he liked them more. He liked to meditate and discovered a knack for transcendence. He liked an Indian holy man called Sai Baba and spent three weeks on his ashram in southern India while sleeping on a cement floor. He liked road trips, surprises and Christmas. And, most of the time, he liked me.

He was a generous man who gave away many of the things he loved. When his best friend Paul died he gave his daughter the treasured medallion Paul had given him after a trip to India. If anyone needed his help, whether it was chopping firewood, discussing dogs or meditation, he was there.

He wasn't a saint; he disliked saintliness as a general principle. He was a man full of complexities that made me pull back in surprise at least once a week. But sometimes I pulled back in hurt and anger because his lack of saintliness, like mine, was based on a sometimes unforgiving need to be right. That need, and an occasional fiery temper that could flare in a moment, led to our first huge disagreement. It came from his decision to stay too long at a friend's home, thereby ruining my painstakingly created dinner (baked arctic char and asparagus) and his sense that that was unimportant. The lack of saintliness was also based on our mutually fierce need to be autonomous, as well as being half of a loving couple. We never really resolved some of those sinkholes in the yellow brick road we travelled together.

But perhaps stories, after all, are the best way to introduce someone...

Tom the cop

When we first met, Tom was the community relations officer at Twenty-One Division in the heart of southwestern Toronto. His day was spent working with social service agencies, schools and parent groups or resolving the disputes of local residents. These were situations that the uniformed officers were unable to resolve or understand. Their solution was to call on Tom to make sense of it all.

Tom's workload included not only the staple items on the job, like talking to community groups, to high school assemblies, or to parent groups concerned about drugs or pedophiles, but he also dropped in to local agencies on a regular basis. Social workers would sometimes ask him to accompany them on difficult calls.

When there were turf wars between rival community groups, between parents and schools, between neighbours and their fences (or the lack of them), between parents and problematic teenagers, Tom was called in. He listened well, and when he proposed a solution it was often unusual but workable.

One day a frantic young Portuguese woman poured out her story to Tom. She was terrified that her children would die because they had been cursed. Instead of dismissing her, Tom decided to investigate. He discovered, by talking to a local healer in her community, that she and her family had become deeply involved in a religious practice that involved the laying-on of spells and other practices closely akin to voodoo. With that knowledge, he was able to enlist the help of some of the leaders of her community who eventually were able to get the family out of a genuinely dangerous situation.

One day his phone flashed when he was in the middle of a struggle with paperwork; the part of his job he hated the most. It was the end of the month and he was counting on a quiet day at his desk to get caught up. So, when the button on the phone turned red, Tom considered, just for a moment, not paying it any attention. But finally, he picked up the receiver to hear the desk sergeant say the familiar words, "I've got a call I think you should take. This woman has called half-a-dozen times, and I don't have a clue what to say to her."

Soon he was driving down one of the quiet, homely streets of southwestern Toronto. Mrs. Kowalski had been the person on the other end of that phone call and she had sounded upset. Her story was confusing. He reflected later that much of his work could come under the heading of "confusing".

As he pulled up to the neat bungalow with its pretty, old-fashioned flower beds lining the carefully swept sidewalk, he wondered what was going on behind the aluminum storm door and the heavy wooden one behind it. Seconds after knocking, after much unlocking and drawing of bolts, the doors were opened. Tom introduced himself, showing his badge to the woman with the tightly permed grey hair and the voluminous cotton apron with its pattern of cherries and bananas. She examined the badge carefully before letting him in.

A few minutes later they were settled at Mrs Kowalski's kitchen table drinking tea. The old woman looked like a template for the word "grandmother". Tom half expected her to take a tray of freshly baked cookies out of the oven. But Mrs. Kowalski wasn't interested in baking that day. She needed to explain to this nice policeman that her husband was harassing her and she wanted it to stop. Tom's attention was caught and he asked her to explain.

Over another cup of tea, she told him that she kept getting phone calls from her husband in the middle of the night, always starting at about 3:00 a.m. She had called the phone company but she wasn't happy with their lack of concern. Tom made the obvious suggestion; maybe she should unplug the phone before she went to bed at night? Mrs. Kowalski sighed and said she had tried that and it hadn't worked. The phone would ring and ring even when it was unplugged. The phone company had sent a technician over but he had said there was nothing wrong with the phone, and then he just went away.

By then, her hands were sweeping non-existent crumbs from the spotless plastic tablecloth and her lips were folded into a thin line. Tom observed her carefully. He deflected her distress about the phone by asking about her husband—had there been problems with him since they had separated and how long had he been gone.

"Oh," said Mrs. Kowalski. "We've been 'separated' about ten years now. He died in 1981."

Tom put the fragile china cup down carefully. Then, just as carefully, he explained to her what needed to be done. First, he picked up the cups and saucers and put them on the kitchen counter. He told her to get the troublesome phone and bring it to him. Next, she was to get a roll of aluminum foil, some scissors and a ruler. She didn't question him; she just did it.

When all this was assembled on the table and he had her full attention, he explained that what he was about to tell her was known to only a few people. The phone company would be upset if they knew he was giving out this closely guarded secret to civilians, but she was a special case. Mrs Kowalski nodded in anticipation; finally someone would help her.

Tom told her to tear off a sheet of aluminum foil, measure off a piece that would be exactly eight inches by eight inches. It must be folded in half, very carefully. Then, the ends must be folded towards the middle. Finally, the end of the telephone line, the one that went into the jack, must be placed in the middle fold of the foil and wrapped carefully until it was well sealed. When all was done to Tom's satisfaction, the telephone with its foil-wrapped wire was put in a metal cookie tin and placed in a deep drawer.

Mrs. Kowalski gave a great sigh of relief. As Tom got up from the table getting ready to leave, she went to a cupboard and took out a Tupperware container of homemade spice cookies. She called them "hermits". The officers at Twenty-One Division would have homemade cookies with their coffee that afternoon.

The dead husband never interrupted her sleep again. Mrs. Kowalski called Tom a week later to tell him so.

Mrs. Kowalski's telephone was only one of many diverse neighbourhood problems. There were many distraught parents of kids with behavioural, drug or school issues. Tom had many kitchen table meetings with families where he brokered deals between two or three generations. He had an intrinsic authority that even the toughest kids respected. He appeared regularly at the local high school where he could keep an auditorium full of teenagers listening to every word, asking questions and laughing with him. Instead of lecturing them about drugs and alcohol, he told them stories. He kept them a little off balance by alternating comic relief stories about the dumb-ass things people do, with stories about the kids who kill or maim themselves and their friends while drinking and driving. He took it as a personal affront if he couldn't engage the coolest of the Mimico High School students when he spoke to them in their large, drafty auditorium.

He was a friend of frightened and distraught old ladies, impartial arbiter between parents and messed-up kids, as well as a genuinely funny public speaker. But he could also be "Tom the Enforcer" when it came to the bad guys. He was more likely to give a stumbling drunk a ride home on a Saturday night than put him in a jail cell, but if that drunk beat his wife or kids, Tom had no mercy. At midnight, on a lonely city street, he was the arbiter of social justice. He was proud of doing police work and he did it as well and as fairly as he could.

meeting Tom

The first time I met Tom, I had just started a new job at Madeira House, a halfway residence for men convicted of multiple drunk driving offences. Many of the inmates were long-time alcoholics, but some were just stupidly short-sighted.

My job, as program co-coordinator at Madeira, was to facilitate nightly meetings, show films and do individual counselling. A few of the more unrepentant alcoholics felt that the police just had it in for them. One fellow confided that some sorry cop in north Toronto had stopped him twice at the same intersection, both times after he "just had a couple of beers after work". But the third time: "The son of a bitch gave me a summons!"

Luckily, there were others who began the long, painful trip toward knowing that their lives and their family's lives would be ruined if they didn't stop drinking. But many were afraid to change because that would mean losing their drinking buddies who were their only friends. Social life so often revolved around beer.

One morning, after only a week or so of working at Madeira House, I was there alone doing paperwork. When the doorbell rang, I opened the door cautiously—this was a correctional facility after all. Standing there was a man I had never seen before. He had a stocky build, was fairly tall, middle-aged and with the bluest eyes I had ever seen. He wasn't smiling and he wasn't talking. I felt awkward and had no idea what to say. I was supposed to be in charge but I wasn't sure what to do with strange men on the doorstep who looked respectable, but, on the other hand, who knew?

Finally, I said, with a certain amount of caution, "Are you a new resident?"

And then Tom started to laugh, his eyes crinkled and a voice with a still recognizable Geordie accent said, "I'm Tom Brown, Community Relations Officer with Twenty-One Division. You must be the new program person. Pat, isn't it?"

I had no idea what a Community Relations Officer was but I wasn't going to ask. And my embarrassment made it difficult not to sound sulky as I ushered him through the house to my office. Once there, we had coffee, and recognizing my discomfort, he quietly explained what his job was and why he would turn up on the doorstep from time to time.

A few weeks later my boss said, "My, that Tom Brown seems to be spending a lot more time here than he used to."

I just nodded happily and wondered if he was going to join us again for lunch.

We discussed travel, his job, my kids, his daughter, the death of his wife a year or so before, meditation, his recent trip to India and his fascination with Sai Baba, the Indian holy man. How could I resist a cop who had just spent three weeks on an ashram in India?

Like many policemen, especially those of the old school, the world was divided neatly into "good guys" and "bad guys". Tom and I spent a lot of time discussing grey areas, but he could only soften up to a point. After that, his jaw would set and there was no use in talking any more. Sometimes we would laugh and he would call me Miss Grey Area while I would suggest that the black and white police cars were painted the right colours.

The first night I facilitated a group when Tom was to be the guest speaker I didn't know what to expect. I was thinking fox and chickens but not sure which would be which.

I found out soon enough. Tom's relaxed manner, his ability to listen and answer any questions, and his speed in calling the group members on their behaviour when the questions became obnoxious, triggered interest and respect. I was the one on the fringe; they were a bunch of guys sitting around talking about important stuff. I wasn't the program facilitator any more, I was almost invisible, and that was just fine. I enjoyed sitting back and letting the talk and the testosterone roll around me without having to respond in any way at all.

As Tom and I got to know each other away from Madeira House, I learned that there was a small part of him, well-hidden, that felt regret, even inadequacy, because his formal education was so limited. I told him that if he spent even a couple of hours in any graduate department of any university he would radically revise his view of higher education. But the coal miner from the north of England, without a high school education because his parents wanted him to work in the mines when he was fifteen, felt mentally inferior. The evil British tradition of knowing your place and staying there was a stain on his idea of himself that he could never entirely erase.

But those blue eyes of Tom's could see into the heart of things. It made him a good cop and a good man. The compassion and humour behind those blue eyes made me realize one day, as I sipped the god-awful coffee that Madeira served up twenty-four hours a day, that I'd better marry this man. And that, as they say, was that.

Tom came to dinner

But before all that, before the wedding and the geraniums and the blissful, uproarious honeymoon, there were dinners. First, the one at my place.

The house sparkled and gleamed from the most thorough cleaning it had been given for a long time. My two kids had also cleaned up pretty well. Even the resident animals had been threatened with unhappy consequences if they became nuisances. Ben remained visible; first because red meat was on the menu, and secondly, because he recognized a dog person in Tom. The cats had disappeared to their favourite well-hidden places to sleep. One would never know that we even had cats. I looked around and was pleased with my universe.

I had forgotten that pride goeth before many unpleasant surprises. It is the nature of the universe and as constant as the second law of thermodynamics. Or the old Baltimore Catechism.

Nevertheless, dinner went well. It was a safe traditional menu. Steaks, Caesar salad and strawberry shortcake. Jennifer and John kept up their end of the conversation and obviously liked Mom's new boyfriend. While demolishing a large portion of Caesar salad, John informed me, with great delight, that he had met Tom before I did. He had taken a course on law at Mimico High School and Tom had been a popular guest speaker.

As we began eating our steaks, the kids were responding to his humour. He told them the story of how a squad car had been stripped in the parking lot of another high school as the two police officers were inside speaking to the principal. It was also a cautionary tale as he let them know what happened to the students involved in the strip-down.

Jennifer asked him about cops sometimes harassing kids without any good reason. Jennifer, knowing she had a lovely smile, flashed it at him as she asked the question. Tom, also with a smile and his tongue firmly in his cheek, said, "Don't you think some kids need a little harassing?"

I poured myself another glass of wine. For once I was smart enough to be quiet and let the scene play out without any interference. His ability to tell a story held their attention and he talked with them, not at them. The additional fact that this man was sitting down to dinner in their home and romancing their mother was only a moderately weird example of how incomprehensible adults could be. But as we were clearing the table, I caught a look between the two of them that said very clearly, *Maybe Mom has finally found a keeper.*

They knew that their mother was a staunch feminist, supported most left-wing causes, and probably didn't feel that police departments were the most forward-thinking organizations in the world. Just as I had learned that Tom didn't fit into any stereotypical image of a policeman, John and Jennifer discovered that for themselves over dinner that night. (Much later, John began calling Tom "P.C. Dad".) That night they heard stories about the strange and wonderful side of policing the lakeshore area, but they also heard about his recent trip to India and his three weeks in an ashram.

The evening went well and the children disappeared at an appropriate time. Before Tom left, I asked him if he wanted to walk the dog with me. Being a dog lover, he readily agreed. What he didn't realize was that Ben's nightly walk included his housemates, the five cats who followed "Ben the Protector" every night.

The nightly ritual on Eighth Street usually took place around 11:00 p.m. and passing cars were known to stop to watch the procession. I suppose we were quite a sight, but being so used to it, it never occurred to me to pay much attention. Ben was always on a lead held by one of the two-footed members of the household; Henry, the eldest cat, was a rather heavy set, worried old girl who set off on these walks with determination but also great trepidation. She never made it past Morrison, the first cross-street, since that obviously was the end of the known world. Then she would sit on the curb and meow piteously until the procession returned. Molly, the next in age, and a drama queen, was brave enough to go to the middle of the next block. But she made us aware of the danger and her own bravery by suddenly stopping in mid-stride and yowling. That would do it for the other three cats. They would skulk under parked cars with Molly and wait for the parade to pick them up on the return pass.

That night, Tom allied himself with Henry and the first cross-street became his limit too. As we stood on the corner, surrounded by the five cats and a large dog straining at the leash, a squad car from Twenty-One Division suddenly pulled up beside us. Tom's embarrassment became evident when the two uniformed officers leaned out of their windows, both of them laughing so hard they could barely speak.

"Well Tom," one of them said. "Is cat walking a new paid duty for you?"

Tom was a kind, gentle, well-respected man but he was still a cop with cop friends. They had been polite about his trip to India and only the odd person risked his wrath by making a wisecrack about it, but walking cats was fair game. He knew that it would be a long time before this incident would be forgotten.

When we returned home, Tom was very quiet and left shortly afterwards. I felt distressed at his apparent embarrassment. All my feelings of joy about a lovely evening were disappearing.

But I should have known better. He called the next day, his voice full of laughter, wondering when the next parade would be. My worry that five cats had ruined a lovely evening and a budding relationship was blown away.

A few days later, Tom called and asked me to his place for a home-cooked dinner. He wanted to show me that he could cook too. Of course I agreed. A few minutes later, the phone rang again. Tom said that he was planning the menu but had come up against a small problem. "I know you like wine," he said, "but I don't know what colour to materialize." That stopped me in my tracks: materialize? What was he thinking? Then I remembered his stories about the trip to India and how some of the holy men were capable of producing or "materializing" a substance called *verboti* out of thin air. I was curious; we had had an interesting conversation about the strange and wonderful phenomenon that was India.

So as I listened to his voice on the phone talking about wine colour and materializing things, laughter just beneath the surface, I felt my heart leap, it truly felt like a leap of pure joy, and then I laughed until I had to sit down. I could hear Tom's bellowing laugh through the phone line. Later, when I put the handset back on its cradle, very carefully, I was still smiling. I sat on the edge of the chair, in blessed stillness, for a long time. When I stood up, I knew that this man would be in my life forever.

It seems that there is a kind of laughter that is transcendent. It takes us out of the ordinary world of chuckles and funny stories into a world where, just for a moment, the pure joy of being alive and fully conscious is almost more than we can bear. It takes us to the limit of being human, and perhaps, even a little beyond.

another dinner

I believe the menu was minced and mashed at that first dinner, Tom's default cooking option. This simple but delicious meal came after the phone call about wine colour, when laughter gave reality a nudge.

I dressed carefully for this dinner and left extra time for a short detour. I stopped at our neighbourhood florist, down the street from Frank's Fashions. In that damp and fecund place I scanned the pots and bins and coolers that were full of the lushness and brilliant colours that matched my mood. Back in a corner of one of the refrigerators full of roses I spied a glowing burst of golden orange. It was a perfect bud, just beginning to be full blown. It was numinous with presence and spoke of love and longing and spirit. That was the one I bought, the one I presented to Tom as he handed me a glass of red wine, newly "materialized" from the local liquor store.

After dinner, over another glass of wine, we talked about our travels. I told him about taking my kids on a trip through Spain and Portugal a few years earlier. Tom told me a story about taking his daughter Lora to England. They spent a few days in London before travelling north to spend time with his family. On returning to their hotel one evening, Lora discovered that her first period had arrived. No comforting mother, no friends, no supplies, only her Dad. Lora, in tears and embarrassment, explained her predicament. Tom went back out into downtown London, found an open drugstore and bought what he knew Lora would need.

When he returned, he found that Lora had stopped crying, but the clothes she had worn were saturated with menstrual blood. Tom told her to put on pyjamas and settled her in front of the television. Then he ran water in the bathtub and scrubbed the clothes until they were clean. The next day they set off for the north of England.

Much as I hate to admit it, I was unnerved. This was not a subject I had previously discussed with men so soon into a friendship. The sudden discomfort I felt as he got into the story, that to him was simply an interesting travel experience, made me realize that just when you think you have left the social rules of polite conversation and rules of conduct for refined women behind, something crops up to say: *See, here's another bump in the road to liberation that you weren't expecting.* Tom was further along that road than I was.

This story has stayed with me through the years not only because of what Tom was able to do for his daughter, but that he was so comfortable with the telling. This was life happening; you coped and you got on with things. At the time, I felt a stirring of recognition that this, the telling of true stories without ego and without embarrassment, was a quality I had always been looking for. Without ever naming the quality, without even knowing that such a simple truth was at the heart of a woman's search for her man.

and then there were four

I met Judy when she was still married to her first husband, a man they called Duke, although I never understood why. (Perhaps the same backwards logic resulted in the biggest Wolfhound I ever knew being called Mouse). Duke was a colleague when we both worked for a publishing house we unaffectionately called "Carrion Press".

When he introduced me to Judy, the marriage was on its last shaky legs and I discovered that I liked Judy rather more than her husband. Our friendship was cemented during many agonized telephone conversations about how unhappy she was and how wicked he was. One night, she said, probably for the third time, "If only I could make him understand!"

I was tired, it was very late, and I wanted to go to bed. "So how long are you going to give him to understand: week, a month, 20 years?"

She left the next week.

Some years earlier, Judy had met a lovely man called Derek. They hadn't seen each other for four years but a connection had been made. Sometimes the universe unfolds in spectacularly serendipitous ways. Derek called her within weeks of her leaving Duke. Unknown to Judy, his marriage had also ended.

These two refugees from marital war zones began a courtship that made everyone around them remember what it was like to be romantically in love. Some of us surveyed our own romantic wasteland and became wistful. They were like teenagers who had just discovered sex and for a brief time, were oblivious to the rest of the world and its problems. They were also like two puppies and I was happy for them. But unfortunately, I didn't have a puppy. My happiness for them was sometimes tempered by loneliness.

Judy and Derek bought a tiny perfect house in New Toronto. They were married there and gained custody of Derek's two children. Seven months later I bought another of those tiny perfect houses on Eighth Street. The three of us shared many meals and wine-filled evenings swatting mosquitoes in our back yards. We were struggling with the perplexities of raising pre- and adolescent children as well as other vicissitudes of life. Eighth Street was a good place to do it. Its leafy stillness and off-beat inhabitants gave it a homey, peculiar, charm.

Then, in the middle of an ordinary October workday, Tom came into my life. All of a sudden there were four of us. As Tom and I got to know each other (and shared a few dinners) it became time for him to meet my friends. Derek and Tom liked each other right away; they had both emigrated from the north of England as young men so they had common ground. When they talked of things like chip butties (french fry sandwiches to us) Judy and I turned up our Canadian noses. Tom and Derek just laughed. To hear Derek laugh was one of life's joys; it started in his gut and was raucous enough to have every head in a movie theatre turn his way. Since my sense of humour verges on the smartass, I often said things that tickled his fancy. Sometimes I would deliberately think of something funny to say just to hear him laugh.

In 1988 when Tom and I bought a cottage on a Haliburton County lake, we spent an increasing amount of time at it. Tom retired shortly afterwards and I was able to condense my work-week into three days. But one day we realized that I was working largely to support a life in a city where we really didn't want to be. The decision to live full time in cottage country almost made itself.

In 1990, Derek and Judy bought a piece of land nearby, built a log cottage and began the weekly trek north. Almost every weekend the four of us would gather for lazy afternoons on the water and great dinners with wine, new generations of mosquitoes and again, much laughter. We talked each other through the worries we had about our children's marriages, divorces and pregnancies. We survived illnesses and financial concerns. We discussed our worries about the state of the world and the state of Haliburton County. And always, in the midst of everything, Derek's laughter endured.

A few years ago, at the age of sixty, Derek was diagnosed with cancer of the oesophagus. Many years before Tom had discovered and developed an ability to help people who were in pain. He used his version of therapeutic touch to relieve suffering to a degree that I always found astonishing. He made several trips to the city to soothe Derek's pain and anxiety. There were surgeries, many tests and treatments. For a while things seemed well. But the cancer spread through his body and on New Year's Day, 2005, Derek died and the world was changed for all who knew him.

At his memorial service Keith, his brother-in-law and comrade in laughter, asked all of us to close our eyes and think of Derek. When we opened them, Keith said, "Every one of you was smiling because when you thought of Derek did you not think of him laughing? And didn't that make you smile?"

At the end of that day, Tom and I drove home full of the heaviness that comes with the loss of someone special. But we remembered Keith's words and we remembered the sound of laughter—it is a fine legacy Derek. And one I had cause to remember on the day we said goodbye to him at the top of a hill on a cool, windy day in Glastonbury, England.

To Derek

You loved my irreverence Derek.
You laughed at me, that rudely raucous cackle
that let us know exactly where you were,
from three streets away.

When we spread your ashes
in Glastonbury
the wind took them and spread them,
not just on the billowing daisies,
but on the jacket of a grieving friend.

That pale sprinkle caught her
just as she embraced the grieving widow, saying
with pious love,
"He will always be with us!"

And I, hypnotically staring
at flecks of grey ash,
unable to stop myself,
said, "Yes he will.
As long as you don't wash your jacket."

When I stood appalled,
waiting for the lightening bolt, or at least
a malignant stare,
I heard you laugh Derek—that rudely raucous cackle
and it healed the hurt, the loss,
the unutterable sadness
of that day in a Glastonbury meadow.

Eighth Street: one door closing

It was a warm August day in 1987 and I was leaving Eighth Street almost seven years to the day after I had moved there. Derek and Judy stood on their front porch hands waving in slow arcs that looked like salutes. I couldn't open the car window to wave back because Jennifer had lost her grip on the two nervous cats in her lap and one was howling in the vicinity of my right ear.

Today was our moving day and this was the last load to be delivered to Jennifer's new home. Tom had left an hour before with an overloaded van carrying my belongings to his, and now our, apartment. My grown-up daughter was moving into a rooming house on Palmerston Avenue with other student nurses. My son John had already moved into his very own place on Margueretta Street (with much of the Eighth Street furniture).

A quick glance in my rear-view mirror, looking about halfway down the block, showed me a small, neat-looking red brick house. My house that was. It was narrow, but just right for the size and shape of the lot. Mr. and Mrs. Archer, the original owners, were wise when they built it in 1917 because they left space for a driveway and a garage. They knew that the Model T they had been admiring for months would soon be theirs and it would need a proper berth. The long narrow driveway between my house and the next had given me pause more than once since my current car was somewhat wider than a Model T.

The house had weathered the years with stoicism and even some grace in spite of its plainness. My contributions, a new solid front door

38

that I had painted a very dark green and the new casement windows across the front porch, didn't seem to detract from its integrity. I had planted a few perennials in the front garden but they couldn't compare with the rose bushes bought by the Archer children on successive Mother's Days and now over fifty years old. One of those gifts was an old peace rose that signalled the start of summer every year with its soft curling buds of delicate pink and rose. All the rosebushes bloomed every summer and were more fragrant than their descendants.

I stopped at the top of the street before turning right onto Lakeshore Boulevard. I looked out the passenger window at the corner store run by the Korean family who took it as a personal affront if they didn't have what you were looking for in their cluttered but efficient store. Beside them was the tiny shop with the large sign advertising the sale of "Big Gods and Little Gods". Frank's Fashions still had its colourful window display of dusty polyester blouses, ladies handbags, track suits and flannel pyjamas. Frank had disappeared from the scene long ago and the ancient cash register was now presided over by a skinny grey woman—she had grey skin and hair and wore a long grey cardigan. She always had a cigarette drooping out of one corner of her mouth, meaning conversation was difficult and parcel wrapping somewhat dangerous.

Looking behind me again, I could still see Derek and Judy waving. As the tears started, I reminded myself that Tom would have returned the moving truck by now and would be waiting for me at the apartment, probably in exhausted relief. My heart lifted for a moment but then settled more deeply into mourning. I had loved this street, that house, those people, that life. Jennifer and John had grown up here and now they were on their way to their own new lives, as was I. But right now, nothing felt exciting or even challenging. It felt like death.

Hours later, I deposited Jennifer in her new home with two loudly complaining cats and a car full of belongings—all of which needed to be carried up two flights of stairs. Jen and I did a bit of unpacking and arranging of belongings. I met her housemates and gave Jen an enveloping hug. A hug that contained all the love and hope and fear that we were both feeling. With tears still dripping onto my filthy t-shirt, I drove to Tom's apartment. Now it was our apartment, our home.

I closed the door and sank down onto the floor in weary exhaustion. I tried to pull this new home around me, to feel its smells, its energy. But it was just empty space. And then a long arm reached down to pull me up from the floor and put a glass of red wine in my hand. "Welcome home," said Tom. "Shall I order a pizza?"

At that moment I could feel the part of my soul that belonged with Tom lifting and greeting and loving. In the next moment I had a sudden, delicious flash of memory—to the first time he had come for dinner to my house on Eighth Street. And I felt myself smiling, remembering his embarrassment when we took a large dog and five cats for a walk, when a squad car stopped and a cop friend asked him about his new "paid duty".

And then, the laughter as well as the memory of that night faded. I was folded into Tom's arms, great arms for bear hugs, and he was murmuring the sweet nothings that I suddenly longed to hear. "Pepperoni? Extra cheese? More wine?"

Part Three
A Honeymoon, Travels and Dogs

snowshoes and Greece

One wintry day recently, I thought about planning a trip. If, for example, I were to make prudence a spiritual practice, or just decide to be irresponsible and run up the plastic, I could get away somewhere next winter.

Somewhere that doesn't require boots. Somewhere that doesn't require snow tires and a bag of kitty litter in the trunk in case you get stuck and you need some traction. Somewhere that knuckles don't turn white because the falling snow is so thick you sometimes lose the road until you see pale yellow lights coming towards you through that vortex of swirling snow. Somewhere the word "layers" is used to make a fashion statement—as opposed to here in the semi-frozen north where layers must be worn to prevent frostbite and the onset of bone-chilling cold. None of those layers, starting with serviceable long underwear and ending with nose covering scarves and wind-proof parkas, could in any sense be called fashionable.

There are people who actually revel in this climate. They merrily bundle up as they prepare for a healthy snowshoeing jaunt across the frozen fields. They proclaim, tiresomely, to all who can't avoid listening, "Isn't winter wonderful! I just love this season!" It makes me want to smack them up the side of their helmeted heads.

Perhaps a mid-winter break would make me feel less toxic toward the white season. I could stay around long enough to appreciate the admittedly admirable qualities of snow clad pine trees, children skating on frozen lakes, snowflakes large as saucers settling on my tongue and tasting of purity.

But, I digress. If I continue in that vein I will find myself pulling on my boots and walking naked into the large snowbank blocking my driveway. Or signing up for snowshoeing lessons. Or even writing a poem about the taste of snow.

So next winter I might dig my bare toes into warm sand, feel ocean breezes caress sun-warmed skin, turn the pages of a bestseller and wonder what form of finned or shelled sea creature would be on the lunch menu. Then, after the required siesta, I would walk along dusty (snowless) streets inhaling the sights and smells and sounds of a culture steeped in sunshine and the smell of the sea. Somewhere with olive groves, good wine (or even not so good), cypress trees and white houses with tiled roofs. Greece, Italy or perhaps the soft red cliffs of the Algarve.

But today I sit here by the window staring at snow slanting down from the north. There is a travel brochure in my lap full of pictures with a lot of blue and gold in them. Maybe next year.

Meanwhile, this land, this difficult and beautiful place, draws me in. It is now part of who I am. It is where I choose to live. It is all around me, it has formed how I see and hear and understand the larger world. It is home. So I am allowed to complain. Perhaps next year I will visit Greece. I will sit on a sandy beach watching the blue sky and I will probably dream of snowshoes.

I will also dream of a trip to Greece that I made with Tom twenty years ago. I will explore some of the ports of call we made on the cruise that was our honeymoon. I will re-visit places that we enjoyed together and I will remember, with pain and longing, how it was to travel with a companion so close to my heart. But I will also visit new places and create new memories.

Maybe we are here on this lonely planet, kicking cans, shovelling snow and having adventures so that we can create memories and stories to amuse God on lonely nights in a Heaven where snow falls but you don't need long underwear or snowshoes. A place where the cold is academic and snow-shovelling theoretical. I'm not in heaven, may never be, but Tom, in case you're listening, if I haven't annoyed you with this rant about snow, listen while I tell you and anyone else up there who needs a story, about the two weeks on the Mediterranean that was our honeymoon.

after the geraniums:
the best (and only) honeymoon I ever had

"Pudding or cake? What you want?"

The young Greek waiter shifted uneasily from one foot to another.

"We want both," said Tom with a grin.

"Two desserts for you?"

"No, no," said Tom waving his arm expansively. If we had been characters in a B movie he would have had a cigar in his hand. "We want double desserts all around."

This was a Greek ship and the waiter pondered this for a moment, scanning his basic knowledge of English, not sure if he had heard it right. Then a smile split his face and he said, "I bring both. For all of you. Lots of both!"

From that night on, we had double dessert every night and a waiter who found us hilarious. Tom was in his glory because like many Brits who lived through the war years as children, he had an insatiable sweet tooth.

Earlier that evening, after locating our cabin, unpacking and checking out the layout of the ship, we went up to the top deck. The lines had been cast off just a few minutes before, and as the dock slipped away behind us, we found deck chairs far up in the prow. The ship made its stately way down the grand canal of Venice, toward the open sea just as the setting sun touched the horizon. I then understood the impulse of heroines in melodramas to pinch themselves to see if

46

they were dreaming. Part of my mind was lost in the beauty and the stillness of the moment, the other part of that same mind, never truly lost, was thinking, *Wow. Someone has really stage-managed this well!* But stage-managed or not, we spent a glorious hour up there in that narrow vee of the ship—glorious not just because of the scenery, but because it was the first time we had relaxed and been by ourselves since leaving home twelve hours before.

Dinner on the first night of the cruise had its magical moments. We met our table companions and exchanged the first of many, somewhat edited versions of our life stories. We watched Venice fading away behind us and we watched familiar stars emerge over the Mediterranean. But I was tired. Glancing at Tom's face, I could see the effects of the past week's activities creasing his face. It had been a tiring week; we had been married only a few days and were still shyly getting used to saying, "my husband" and "my wife".

So much had happened since those first days at Madeira House when we discovered how we shared a deep interest in meditation and eastern philosophy. We had talked and talked and talked—over coffee, over tea, and over the many dripping California sandwiches we both loved and that he sometimes brought for lunch.

One thing eventually had led to another and one day, many months later, he said, "Do you have a medical and dental plan?"

I said, "No, that is one of the disadvantages of agency work."

"Well," said Tom. "That isn't right. I think we should get married and then we could share my plan."

I had heard of many odd marriage proposals, but that was one of the oddest. After a lot of laughing and more of one thing leading to another, we went shopping for a ring. I tried to brush aside the need for a ring, but as far as Tom was concerned, if you were going to do something, you do it right. And if you are going to get married that involves a proper engagement ring. And if you are English, a sapphire is the proper choice. So I was given the beautiful ring with a navy blue stone that looks like the deepest part of the ocean.

A few weeks earlier I had, temporarily, started to smoke again, blaming it on the excitement of planning a wedding. Perhaps blowing clouds away for our wedding made me feel that my lungs were invincible. Tom was a dedicated non-smoker so he wasn't happy about my taking up a new (old) habit, but since we were both in the slightly besotted stage of middle-aged love; he held his peace, at least until after the honeymoon. Besides, we were placed at a smoking table in the dining room which meant that we were introduced to some delightful new (smoking) friends.

The six of us were seated at a round table placed under two portholes which looked out on the darkening sea. Our companions were Barb and Susan, attractive, single, funny and smart who were travelling together to shake recent divorces out of their hair. Ron and Sandy had been married about ten years and were on their first big holiday. He was one of the funniest people I had ever met and she was a lovely but more sedate kindergarten teacher and a great foil for his humour. We ate together every evening for two weeks and always, laughter exploded from that table. The first night we were all excited and just a little apprehensive about the cruise. We would be spending thirteen days at sea and visiting places that had only existed in books and fantasies: Venice, Athens, Corfu, Rhodes, Alexandria, Cairo and Jerusalem. I felt like a nineteenth century adventurer clutching safe, middle-class perceptions to my breast but almost ready to let them go if someone asked me nicely.

Tom was much more widely travelled than I. He had lived in the Middle East for two years as part of a United Nations peacekeeping force. Sitting at that round table night after night with our new friends, Tom regaled us with stories of his trading days. One of his jobs when he was posted to Egypt was to ride into the desert to trade coffee for fresh eggs with the Arabs. He told us of the canniness of the Bedouin who would generously offer tea after the trading and haggling had been done. Then he would surreptitiously cover some of Tom's eggs with his robes all the while chatting politely. Gimlet-eyed Tom, while keeping up his end of the conversation, would pull the eggs back from under those voluminous robes. Neither man would acknowledge the by-play. Both smiled and bowed and went away happy. Tom because he had got his eggs back, the Arab because he had managed to hide a couple more that he had pushed even further under the robe.

He told us about Christmas Eve in the desert when they drove out over the dunes under a full moon and built a huge bonfire in a sandy valley. They drank beer and sang Christmas carols under the stars until dawn came. Tom was able to make us feel the poignancy of that night as a group of solitary men came together to sing and remember other Christmases in other lands with other companions.

Many of the stories we told each other at that round table were funny, and often enlightening, or they seemed so at the time. Serendipity does bring spirits together in unlikely settings so that they become kindred for a time and then drift away, back into a normalcy that was suspended for a time. So the six of us spent many hours eating mediocre food and worse wine but somehow present and mindful of every moment. Sometimes we would laugh so hard at each other's stories that we would get unfriendly stares from the other tables. But we were beyond caring. Like two long-in-the-tooth teenagers adrift in their own world, we were having an adventure, and the niceties of sedately polite society didn't have much impact.

But that first night, sitting at the round table that would be the scene of many raucous meals, I glanced out the porthole over Barb's right shoulder. The last trace of the glowing sunset had faded and the darkness was complete. Tom and I decided to go back on deck rather than go to the after dinner cabaret. We managed to find our way again to the top deck and sat on a wooden bench holding hands in the stillness, watching the stars align themselves in the old familiar patterns. It didn't matter that neither of us could identify much more than the Big Dipper. The beauty of a starlit sky had the same magnetic pull as it did for the astronomers, ancient and modern, who wondered, with awe and humility: *Does anything lie beyond?* But that night we didn't ponder the great astronomical and spiritual questions of the ages. We were too intensely present in that splendid and fragile moment.

The next morning, in the soft pre-dawn light, those of us too excited to sleep stood in the prow of the ship (the pointy end as Tom had explained to the nautically challenged Ron). As the greyness gradually lightened and the ship pulled closer to our first port of call, the island of Corfu, Tom and Ron were busy fiddling with their expensive single lens reflex cameras. They both cautioned me that it was still too dark to take pictures. But I raised my little $50 Konica and took a few shots of purpled hills rising from a deep blue sea. When the film was developed a few weeks later, the mist, the fragile quality of the light, were captured by that little camera. That ethereal quality would have disappeared with sunrise. An early lesson in marital bliss, listen respectfully and then do what you need to do.

There were other beautiful Greek islands, all calling us to stay a while longer, maybe a lifetime. The hilly, narrow streets of Rhodes where we bought a second fragile and intricately carved wedding ring, one that actually fit. The dry, dusty island of Crete where ancient history was more real than it had ever been in a classroom. The tavernas that jutted into the sea where lemonade never tasted better. But we were staunch Canadians; all that decadent sunshine and toasted beaches had to be sinful. Mind you, if the ship's bell hadn't been clanging reminding us of other ports to come, we might very well have decided to be sinful.

After regretfully leaving those luscious islands filled with laughter and wine and golden light, our ship sailed onwards, across a choppy sea to Port Said, our entrance to the land of the Pharaohs, the pyramids and cheap perfumed oils.

Perhaps because of his experience with the Bedouins, Tom relished the art of haggling and no matter where you were in the Middle East, haggling was an art form. Initially, I couldn't get the hang of it; I kept thinking of the poverty in these countries. It would be like stealing from the church poor box. That was before I understood the somewhat intricate rules of the game. And before I walked away from a disappointed vendor, saying, in my typical apologetic Canadian fashion, that the price was too high for me. That's when Tom took over my education. Under his tutelage, I became quite adept. In fact, by the time we left Turkey I was able to leave a shop keeper wringing his hands before I made him laugh at his own melodrama. I walked away with a beautiful leather bag at a great price. At least I think I did. One never knows for sure and the shopkeeper looked pretty happy when we left the store.

Tom really hit his stride at the outdoor market at the docks in Port Said. As we hurried up the gangplank, the ship's bell clanging in annoyance at our tardiness, I saw one bearded Arab with a huge grin on his face waving good-bye to his new friend Tom, while another shook his head and looked disconsolately at his depleted wares. Tom was chortling and admiring one more item destined for what I called his tacky shelf. This shelf, in an unobtrusive hallway of our home, held souvenirs and mementos of our trips. Much of it was quite trashy but Tom loved every item sprawling across the top of an otherwise respectable book shelf. His new treasure, an over stuffed leather camel with gaudy markings would join the wondrous Eiffel tower, the dancing Indian woman and the glass enclosed piranha from Columbia.

One night, later in the cruise, we decided to organize the gifts we had haggled so diligently for—gifts to ourselves as well as to others. All our sorting and organizing took a little longer than we had expected so when we were late coming down for dinner, our four friends decided to come and pick us up. When we opened the door, there they were, grinning broadly. "Just checking to see what the honeymoon couple was up to," said Ron with a leer that would have done Groucho Marx proud. They crowded in and we had a neighbourly drink before leaving for dinner. They were astounded at the size of our cabin which we considered comfortable but minuscule. "My God, they could both get dressed at the same time. We have to take turns," said Barb.

From that night on, they insisted that in order to have such luxury we must have shares in the company that owned the ship. Tom went along with the gag. He told them that yes, they had found us out. We were on a secret mission to make sure that the ship was being run properly and to his satisfaction. Anytime something was found to be not quite up to standard (his), Ron would complain to Tom who would immediately pretend to make a note and promise that he would see to it. Our elevated position, in reality due to our honeymoon status and early booking, became the source of a lot of laughter and bad jokes.

Later, the emotional earthquake that was Jerusalem—its solemnity disturbed only by our visit to the Church of the Holy Sepulchre where Christ was apparently entombed. We were waiting in the middle of a long, snaking line when some poor sod cracked his head on the top of the solid stone entrance to the tomb. Simultaneous with the sound of that crack, was his unthinking and pain-filled yell, "Jesus Christ!"

At the end of the long line, a voice was heard to slowly intone, "Yeeess?"

Memories come crowding back: the frightening camel ride where only Tom's strong arms kept me from sliding ignominiously down the long slope of camel neck into the sand; the afternoon in Giza, as I lay on my back, floating peacefully in the hotel pool and lazily opened my eyes to see the Pyramids, so close that I unconsciously raised my arm as though to touch them.

Tom and I travelled to many places over the years, always with a sense of exploring the unfamiliar, whether it was hiking into the jungle in Venezuela or, a cheap quick holiday, flying anywhere that didn't require parkas and boots.

Our mighty ship, The Jupiter, sank a few months after we returned home to Toronto. So the arrival of a condolence card from Ron on the loss of "our" ship, brought us back to those days of laughter, sunshine, blue seas, white houses with tiled roofs, steep hills covered with fragrant pine trees, and all those other cliché sights and sounds that make you understand why they became clichés.

after the honeymoon

Returning home after two weeks on the Mediterranean took some adjusting of perspective. One of those adjustments concerned the matter of smoking. Beginning a new life, in a new home with my new (relatively) love, required this commitment. There were a couple of false starts, but one day, with a little bit of help, it took.

That day was the first beautiful, spring day. Warm and sunny...

travelling music

Approaching the car, I heard an ear bending blast of music as The Boss belted out "Born In The U.S.A." The car's engine was running; Tom's hands were tapping the steering wheel and his face was creased with joy. I slammed the door as I got in the car, threw my bag on the backseat and planted a large, wet kiss in the vicinity of his right ear. And then we were off. So many of our travelling adventures began with the pounding rhythm of Bruce Springsteen's anthem. That day, "Me and Bobby McGee" was the follow-up as we rolled along Highway 401 heading east.

Later, as the miles flashed by and we settled into the rhythm of the trip, the mellow sounds of Willie Nelson filled the car. And of course, there was plenty of Kristofferson—the guy who could make Tom forget that he had been a cop for twenty-five years and who could make him remember what "Sunday Morning Coming Down" really felt like.

That morning, we headed east out of Toronto and drove through the peaceful roads of Prince Edward County. By then, Willie was soothing us with "Georgia On My Mind" but when it finished, I was still not soothed. Unconsciously, my hand kept reaching into pockets looking for that familiar cardboard pack that wasn't there. My mouth was craving the taste of tobacco smoke and my whole body was strung as tight as a guy-wire.

This was only the second day of self-chosen torture, and already I was composing essays to myself (and to Tom) stating why this reckless plunge into abstinence could not work. Maybe later when the world settled down, maybe after work becomes less pressured. Maybe bloody well NEVER.

The night before this trip, in the small hours of the morning, I had crept out of bed. I stealthily found jeans and a shirt, pulled them on and then tiptoed out of the bedroom. And then the voice, "Where are you going?"

I chose bravado rather than cringing shame. "I'm going out to buy some cigarettes. I can't do this." Before I hit the bedroom door, Tom was out of bed, his sweat pants were pulled on and his arms were around me. By then the tears had started and the sobbing was only seconds away. They were tears of frustration and anger and despair. I didn't think it would be this hard or that I would be this weak. Tom understood. He said, "Let's just sit and talk. I'll make you a drink then decide what you want to do. Do you want a nice cup of tea or booze?" He looked at me. "Booze it is."

So we sat down at the kitchen table with a bottle of Canadian Club between us. Tom had one drink and then made himself a pot of tea. He wasn't much of a drinker and he knew he had a job to do. I finished that first drink and then the second as I burbled on about how hard this was, how smoking had become not only my crutch but my friend. How it was when I looked in the mirror and saw a coffee and cigarette person, not a herbal tea drinking wimp (real women drink boiled coffee and roll their own tampons). By the third drink I realized that I couldn't drive myself to an all night convenience store for cigarettes and knew the answer I would get if I asked Tom. And besides, as I groggily realized, I wanted to sleep even more than I wanted a cigarette.

Tom, by the way, was able to dine out for months on this story of how he helped me to stop smoking by getting me drunk. He and all our friends thought it was pretty funny. Eventually, I was able to join in the laughter but it took a while.

The next morning we both slept in. Over breakfast, when Tom saw the beginning of panic as I faced morning coffee without a cigarette, he suggested a road trip. Maybe east to that provincial park on the shore of Lake Ontario called Sandbanks. The sun was shining and the temperature for a mid-April day was almost tropical.

So that afternoon we walked and talked along the hard-packed sand, watching the waves and the seagulls, greeting the brave souls stretched out on the sand who were gratefully lifting their pasty faces and pink toes to the sun. I have often thought that there is a peculiarly Canadian facial expression in early spring when the surliness of late winter has finally passed and the first promise of life without snow boots has manifested. It is a look of bemused foolishness and vulnerable, bare-naked hope.

I'm sure that same look settled on our faces as we greeted those other faces and toes. And I guiltily wondered if any of them had a cigarette.

Driving home, we listened to the plaintive music of Willie and Kris, music that honoured sadness, despair, and addictions. I was right there, full of empathy and massive self-pity as I missed my friendly pack of cigarettes and flashy red lighter. Then I looked over at Tom, proud of me for making it through two whole days without a smoke. I slipped "The Boss" into the tape deck and settled back to listen to "Born In The U.S.A." one more time.

sunrise at San Jose

Tom and I discovered early in our relationship that we shared more than an interest in meditation and eastern religions. We found that we were passionately interested in two other things: travel and dogs.

One year, before the dogs, but still early in the marriage, we decided to take a break from the back end of a particularly cold and dreary Canadian winter. So, after many evenings poring over travel brochures, we flew south to Los Cabos, Mexico.

In the late eighties, Los Cabos had not yet become popular. It was still peaceful—two fishing villages joined by a magnificent twenty-mile stretch of golden sand beach and huge, rolling breakers. There were only four hotels, well-spaced, along the San Jose end of the beach. We stayed at the smallest and newest of these four. The staff had been recently recruited and what they lacked in finesse, skill and basic English they made up for in good humour, friendliness and a sometimes misplaced helpfulness. Ordering a meal was an adventure that involved many gestures, drama and good will.

Our hotel room was on the ground floor facing east; the ocean was almost at our front door.

At 6:15 A.M. the little travel alarm shrilled in my ear. I opened one eye as I pressed down the lever on the clock and watched light seeping around the edge of the heavy hotel room drapes. I glanced beside me at my still sleeping husband. Gentle, breathy snores were emanating from somewhere under the tumbled sheets. Stealthily, I swung my legs over the side of the bed and pulled on a pair of shorts. The t-shirt could stay on. I decided against sandals; they might make a noise slapping against the tile floor. Grabbing the camera from the dresser and pulling the strap over my head, I inched my way over to the sliding glass doors.

Chortling quietly to myself, I opened the door slowly, just a few inches at a time. I had one foot on the stone patio and was reaching behind me to close the door when a large paw grabbed the back of my shorts and pulled me back into the room.

"Oh no you don't," said the deep voice attached to the paw. "I'm coming too."

"You were playing possum weren't you?"

Tom's answer was a quiet chuckle as he pulled on his shorts and grabbed his own camera. We were ready to leave.

Ever since we had arrived three days before to this beautiful spot where the desert met the Sea of Cortez, we had developed a good-natured but serious competition over who could take the best sunrise picture. I was a new photographer with a cheap camera bought just before the holiday. The little Konica, so useful on our Mediterranean cruise, had disappeared just as I was getting the hang of it. Tom on the other hand, was more experienced and had an expensive Canon to take his well-planned and well-composed pictures. But to my surprise, when we had rushed our first films to be developed at the little shop in town, some of my shots, taken with no regard or knowledge of proper technique, had turned out quite well. But it would have been a little mean if I had managed to get a perfect picture of the perfect sunrise over the perfect beach while Tom still slept.

Holding hands for a moment as we buried our feet in the cool sand, we gazed at the entrancing spectacle which had pulled us out of bed every morning since our arrival in Mexico. The light was becoming luminescent as the dawn streaked an aquamarine sky with deep bands of rose and gold and lavender. The monstrous waves moving towards us were at least eight feet high. When they curled and broke, the spray was a cascade of tiny jewels hurled back onto a sapphire sea.

Meanwhile the sun was just visible at the horizon—a brilliant, white gold disk now at centre stage. Even the powdery sand seemed to glow from that emerging light. The waves reached even higher and the thunder of their breaking should have awakened everyone at the hotel. Yet we were always the only witnesses. When I could stand to turn away, the desert, with its lonely cacti spacing themselves like drunken sentries, stretched as far as I could see. Only the outline of our small, one-storey hotel marked the scene as inhabited.

After a few minutes, we had our pictures and we walked along a beach still deserted and pristine. The sea had begun its day job. Creating a steady, mesmerizing beat, it sent waves that were only a little less tall, crashing to the shore before they slowly ebbed back. Meanwhile, the sun climbed towards a zenith that would dry a wet t-shirt in minutes.

My last picture was of Tom's footprints arching through the sand and then disappearing. Later, that shot would win the prize for best picture of the week (sometimes Tom could admit defeat with an ungrudging generosity). As we walked back to the hotel for breakfast that morning, we didn't know that particular picture would come out so beautifully. So we bickered gently about who had captured the best shot of the day. But neither of us cared very much. We were thinking of breakfast and feeling the now sun-warmed sand between our toes. The weight of Tom's arm around my shoulder was the anchor for all the happiness I had ever known.

After visiting Mexico again and again, after a couple forays into other countries where winter, snow boots and toasted bagels were not available; we flew to a place of jungles, humidity, emeralds and dope smugglers.

winter 1992

"Do you think we might go someplace ordinary next year?

I heard the wistful note in Tom's question. It was almost midnight; we were on a pot-holed dirt road running through the jungles of Colombia and we had been travelling for far too long without sleep. We were on an ancient bus that threatened to break down at every pothole; the air was muggy and the heat oppressive. The people in the bus were starting to smell and I suspected that I might be among them. I was hot, tired, cranky and feeling less and less disposed to foreign travel.

That year, after celebrating Christmas and New Year with family and friends, in the chill of pre-dawn darkness one January morning, we had followed the stars to the airport and boarded a plane bound for Colombia. Since then, we had trudged through three airports and boarded two buses. The ambience had deteriorated with each change.

This latest bus should have been retired a generation ago. When I realized that we had stopped, for the fourth or fifth time, I didn't know whether it was just catching its elderly breath or if the latest pothole had finally swallowed us up. But peering out through the dirty window, I saw uniformed men with guns and surly faces swaggering along the road beside us. One of them was questioning the driver who seemed to shrink in his seat as the questions continued. Another man in uniform boarded the bus and walked down the aisle staring at passengers who were too tired to be properly intimidated. Finally, we were allowed to continue and most people seemed to settle into a watchful doze.

Not being able to doze, I applied myself to Tom's question. This was our third trip to South America: we had travelled to the jungles of Venezuela and Colombia; we had driven in Land Rovers up to their hubcaps in water; we had travelled the Orinoco River in wide dugout canoes and I had even swum in its tea-coloured water. We had grasped each others hands, and I at least had silently said the Gayatri Mantra, with a few Hail Marys thrown in, while we swooped and careened in a tiny bush plane as it flew into a hugely magnificent canyon. We gazed at the splendour of Angel Falls through billowing mists and shreds of cloud. The turbulence lifted us and then gently allowed us to settle long enough to gaze at one of the world's great natural wonders.

We were not the most intrepid of travellers, but we had seen a few things and had some exciting moments. Some of them more enjoyable in retrospect. So when I heard Tom say that maybe an "ordinary" holiday would be worth considering, I gave the idea full attention.

"Like where?" I said cautiously.

"How about Florida?" Tom answered without a pause.

I stared at him. "Florida? That's for old fogeys in Bermuda shorts and white socks. The couples who drive down the I-75 every winter with two baseball caps on the back window: one saying 'The Old Fart' and the other 'The Old Fart's Wife'."

Tom looked at me, without blinking, without smiling. "We wouldn't have to get the hats."

across the pond

We made many trips to visit Tom's family in the north of England. His sister Margaret and her husband Gordon always provided a welcoming and comfortable home base. I discovered to my surprise that northeast England was not an industrial wasteland of closed down coal mines and ancient slag heaps. Many evenings, after our "tea" (often take-away fish and chips) Gordon would take us for a drive through the peaceful countryside.

The roads, much narrower than we were used to, were bordered by leafy hedges with the occasional sheep or cow peering at us with gentle curiosity. A few miles later we would drive through heather covered moors and a few miles after that, barren stretches of sand where tall and grassy dunes bordered the North Sea. Dotted throughout the countryside, often in the middle of nowhere and surrounded by fields, we found country inns with smoke darkened beams, history and good food.

But the best times were when Tom and I could go off together and he could show me not just the sites but his memories. The market square where the Romans had held slave auctions and where, many centuries later, he would meet his girlfriend on Saturday nights. The ha'penny wood where the owner of the property would try to charge a toll of a half penny to anyone crossing through it. And most amazing to me, the miles of beautiful but deserted sand beaches, hidden and protected by dunes and seagrass from the road. Beaches that we had to ourselves except for the circling, noisy gulls, the crashing surf, and the occasional dog walker.

He showed me the grass-covered hills that hid the slag heaps of other times. He showed me the entrance to the pits where he had worked for eight years—in the dark and dangerous spaces along the coal face, hunched over, pick-in-hand, filling the carts pulled by the patient pit ponies. Eight years of scrubbing, unsuccessfully, to get coal dust out of his pores. And always the worry, never expressed, about accidents, about cave-ins.

He spoke little of that place and those years. When I asked if we should visit the recently rebuilt model mining village where everything had been restored the way it had been over fifty years before, Tom had no interest.

And yet Tom loved that land. His face would soften when he spoke of having the smell and sight and sound of the ocean in his front yard. He showed me the postcard pretty road that meandered along the coast and connected the villages, the route he would take on his bike after the Saturday night dance in the next village. He showed me the spot on the road where he missed a turn and found himself sprawled on the roadside covered with cuts and bruises while his pride and joy, a brand new motorcycle, careened off in the other direction.

Tom's roots went deep into that countryside, but luckily for me, he had been able to grow new tendrils into his adopted country, the one we both called home. And perhaps his accent, a hybrid that had become unrecognizable by anyone on either side of the Atlantic, reflected that reality. It spoke of both places. I was pleased that the broadness of his accent had mellowed. We might never have survived our first conversation if it hadn't.

The Geordie accent of northeast England can be almost incomprehensible to the untutored ear (which is any ear not resident there). But most people, when dealing with foreigners, and that would be anyone living south or west of Newcastle, would kindly adopt what they called "polite" Geordie. Polite Geordie was a toned down, slower version of their everyday speech. But even that was a challenge to my Canadian ears. One night, almost two weeks into our stay, we were watching a television program featuring a much-loved, local comedian. He had the broadest accent I had ever heard. And yet, I heard myself laughing helplessly and understanding almost everything he said. It was probably time to go home.

Two years later, in 2000, we finally made a trip to Ireland and Tom discovered that he enjoyed that country and its people. He felt a little sheepish that it had taken us so long to get there in spite of my pleading. He worried that southern Ireland would look unkindly on an Englishman after enduring so many years under the boot of England. He worried that "the troubles" were of such recent history that he would be unwelcome.

But we discovered that Ireland in the mid-nineties was prosperous, proud and largely indifferent to where its tourists came from. Some of the people we met who worked in hotels and restaurants came from the north of England.

We often laughed when someone would try to puzzle out where Tom came from based on an accent worn down and softened after so many years of living in Canada. Many Irishmen were convinced that he must be Irish, just from another part of the country, maybe down the way, in the next county.

Although we both felt a kinship with that green and welcoming land, a sense of home, we never did make it back for another visit. But the pull was strong, as I suspect it is for many people, even if their ancestors are from Lithuania rather than Wicklow and Cork as mine were.

Mandalas and Dogs

Feeling the sun dissolve the morning chill.
watching the leafy canopy
tremble in the gentlest of gentle breezes,

I am here
mindful of all that,
trying to make a poem.

I'm on the deck,
breakfast is done.
The blue coffee mug sits, pleasantly full, beside me.
The notebook balances on a bare knee; my pen is poised to write.

The dog shuffles over to where I sit,
love in her eyes, drool in her beard.
I lift the notebook away from my knee
I know what is coming.

The dog licks a bare knee and shakes her great head
the bare knee covered with tiny drops of watery drool.
I wipe them away with the end of my shirt.

The dog yawns, collapses beside me with a contented sigh.
Life unfolds. Pleasingly.

I sip my coffee. Replace the notebook on a dry knee.
And begin a poem.

The other dog shuffles over....

for the love of dogs

In 1994 Tom and I packed up our lives and moved to the cottage in Haliburton. After four years of living lives in two places, we had enough of discovering that a favourite shirt or corkscrew had been left at the cottage. Or the book we were in the midst of reading was still on the bedside table at the apartment. Tom had retired by then and I had already squeezed my workload into three days a week so we could spend more time by the lake. One day I sat down with pencil and paper to work out some basic economics. Could we afford to live permanently on Tamarack Lake? I discussed the possibility of change with Tom. The discussion was short. All I can remember of it is: "When should we go?"

Most of our household stuff, and it was a lot since only a few years before we had combined households, we gave away to friends and family. As I watched things moving out the door, there were very few pangs of loss. In the midst of the chaos I felt a sense of lightness and letting go. What we brought with us was either useful or too cherished to be left behind.

This move was a major upheaval from our complicated city lives, but it came with a built in bonus; we would get dogs, big ones, one for each of us. For several years we had lived in an apartment. It was spacious and filled with light, but the front door led to a hallway and the back door to a wide concrete strip called a balcony. We wanted more, and we wanted the more to include dogs.

One day, while browsing in a pet store, we found a video on dog training. Tom had it in hand, on his way to the cashier. He explained the video to me—it used only the very latest and most humane methods in teaching manners to dogs: how to sit, stay and come. Since it was many weeks before we would take ownership of puppies I was a little perplexed.

"Okay," I said. "How will we do this? Take turns being the dog? Will I need a choke chain for you? This is starting to sound a little kinky to me." As other customers stared at us, Tom and I started to laugh hysterically picturing how a dog training session might go without a dog.

Tom had always loved German Shepherds so we carefully researched breeders. We knew that we wanted a puppy bred to be gentle, one with healthy hips and no super-angulated legs. We found the right breeder and a puppy was ordered up. When we first saw him, he was just a tan and black ball of fur with slitty little eyes and a tendency to slide up your chest until he was nestled against your bare neck.

We made two trips to the Niagara Escarpment (an hour's drive south of Toronto) to check on the progress of our growing puppy who could now waddle around on fat little paws. All seemed to be well. When Tom asked for my thoughts on names, I didn't stop to think. "What about Ben?"

He knew the original dog, the loveable slightly neurotic Labrador/ Great Dane cross I had owned when Tom and I first met. We decided to honour "Eighth Street Ben" who had been gone for several years, and hoped that this tiny bundle of furry cuteness would grow into the loving, loyal disposition of that first Ben.

Meanwhile, Tom was free to help me make up my mind on who would be Ben's companion. My choice of a puppy was more complicated. Like a child in a candy store with only one nickel to spend, I couldn't decide on a breed. We went to dog shows and I fell in love with many wonderful dogs. I became a shameless camp-follower, trailing after dogs as their handlers led them away from the show ring. It was an exhilarating time; I met many fine people, breeders who loved their dogs and their breed, as well as those who looked upon dogs as commodities.

During all the searching, one breed haunted me. For weeks we had pored over the big *Dogs in Canada* magazine. We read up on breed descriptions, looked at pictures of puppies, and agonized over the many choices. But there was one picture, a full page shot that almost stopped my heart every time I looked at it. It showed a group of old people seated on lawn chairs outside what was probably a nursing or retirement home.

The sky was blue, the grass was green, the sun was shining, and everyone looked content. Stretched out in the forefront of this bucolic scene, large eyes looking directly at the camera, was the biggest dog I had ever seen. He was a dark grey Irish Wolfhound with a thick wiry coat. He was regal, and he was beautiful. He seemed to be protective of the old people without making a big thing about it (I found out later that his breed seldom makes a big thing out of anything). Something in his expression and his manner said, *I know my place in his world. Don't mess with me!* But those eyes seemed to glow with kindness, intelligence and love. The woman, whose hand rested delicately on his great head, seemed to share my bemusement and delight.

That was a lot to read into one picture in a magazine, but falling in love does not imply logical thinking followed by careful conclusions. The caption beside the picture said his name was Caleb and that he was a "therapy dog" who visited nursing homes with his owner Betty. The article also mentioned his size; he was large, even for an Irish Wolfhound. According to the article, he weighed 180 pounds and stood well over three feet at the shoulder. A huge dog, an animal that belonged to myth, not a living room. Regretfully I closed the book and began another search.

Later that month we decided to go to a dog show held in Toronto. It was a very large show so there would be hundreds of dogs to see and talk to, a great way to spend a Saturday. We arrived early and entered the building through one of its many entrances. As we walked through the double doors, right in front of us was a small booth with a banner on top of it that said "St. John's Therapy Dog Program". In front of that booth was a woman with a large dark grey dog on a leash. He was sitting quietly while allowing a multitude of excited children to pet and hug him. It was Caleb.

Humphrey Bogart's line came to mind, *Of all the gin joints in all the towns.* After the children left, I began a conversation with his owner, Betty, and with Caleb. That conversation has now been going on with assorted Wolfhounds and their owners for many years.

As I walked around the arena that day, admiring and talking to a multitude of dogs and their people, an image of Caleb stayed indelibly printed somewhere behind my eyeballs. My conscious mind was having an intelligent adult conversation with itself: *No sensible person would allow a dog that big into her home. It is far too hairy and far too large. Too much dog altogether.* But underneath that dialogue, my unconscious was chortling happily to itself and thinking of Irish names.

Ryan and me

It was several more months before the puppy who would be Ryan was born. My friend Susan was not having puppies that year since her great white hope Cara, a lovely pale Wolfhound, had decided that she was a radical feminist with lesbian leanings and wanted nothing to do with the male of the species. She refused to get pregnant. So Susan referred me to Lucille and Dunnescroft Kennel in Ottawa. And Lucille *was* having puppies that spring. As anyone who has been through this process, picking a puppy is fraught with stress. The two "pick puppies" were out of the running, they would stay with the breeder, but there were five more squirming, furry bundles to choose from. Luckily for me, the scrawny white one with ears that stuck out at right angles to her head, decided that I would do. I was picked. But choosing a name was another matter.

That day, the one when puppy and person chose each other, was also the day I visited my mother in the hospital and realized that she would not be coming home. Noreen Mary Grace Ryan, aged eighty-six, was far into her long slide into dementia. Mum's maiden name was Ryan; sometimes it is with tears that we recognize synchronicity.

It was a short drive to Dunnescroft Kennel where a litter of Wolfhound puppies were waiting and as I turned into the driveway, the tears on my face had not yet dried. I walked towards the house, and gently let the image of my Mum sink into a deeper level of consciousness, making room for the joyful sight of seven wriggling

Wolfhound puppies just learning how big the world might be and what would be the best way to explore it.

Two weeks later, Ryan and I began a friendship that lasted for five years. We had our moments, both of us being wilful, but as in any good relationship we were able to laugh together. Sometimes we were annoyed with each other, but the annoyance never lasted long. One infamous incident occurred during one of our walks around the lake. I had let her off leash on the cottage road near home. When it was time to get back on leash, she stayed just far enough ahead so that I couldn't quite catch her to snap the lead back on her collar. If I moved faster so did she, always just out of reach. And I know she had a grin on her face when she glanced behind her. But that day I had the last laugh.

Just as she thought we were on the homestretch and she had won, I quickly reached out and grabbed her tail. She was a surprised and indignant Wolfhound, but she knew when she was beaten. She sat docilely while I put on the lead and even had the grace to look a little sheepish.

Ryan's housemate Ben was seven weeks older. They took turns bossing each other around, but when Ben got too pushy, Ryan had the knack of flipping him onto his back before he knew what was happening and then gently fastening her teeth into the loose skin of his throat. She never made a sound, but when he looked sufficiently apologetic, she would let him go and the two of them would be off, running, leaping into the air and then running some more.

Ben and Tom did a lot of obedience training together (sometimes it was hard to tell who was training whom) and Ben was good at chasing after sticks, balls and anything else that was thrown. As Tom liked to say, Ben was a *real* dog. He would even, on occasion, bring things back and stand with tongue lolling, ears pricked high and body tensed with excitement, waiting for the next throw.

Meanwhile, Ryan would watch all this excitement with a Buddhist detachment and dignity. But then mirth would overcome her. Sometimes she would get me to watch the "Tom and Ben Show". Other times she would dance across the deck, all but holding her sides in glee; Wolfhounds seem to have this peculiar ability to express laughter. At the beginning, afraid that Ryan would feel left out while Tom worked or played with Ben, and before I understood the Wolfhound psyche, I would throw a stick for Ryan, making all the appropriate throw-a—stick-for-the dog type noises. Ryan of course, feeling that she was the rightful descendent of Irish queens, would simply look at me in amazement. *You want me to do what? Why did you throw it away if you want it back?*

Ryan was only interested in chasing squirrels, rabbits, and on a really boring day, an obnoxious leaf. Otherwise, exercise consisted in doing laps around the large yard and playing a game with Ben that seemed to involve seeing who could leap the highest into the air without falling over. There were also daily walks and usually we would allow them off-lead. Ben was fast, but soon he would be left behind. Ryan would stretch out those long muscular legs and her face would wear a look of focused joy. In that moment she was grace and beauty and truth and love and death. She was Ryan and I forgave her everything. Especially after an incident that happened one snowy December day.

the ultimate dog story

That morning, shortly after breakfast, I took a sip of hot coffee and began reading the next chapter of my book. The fire in the fireplace was burning well and the deep, comfortable chair was seductive. Lifting my head, I looked out across Tamarack Lake and saw dark clouds building above its leaden surface. The sky seemed darker, more ominous than it had a few minutes earlier. But a large stack of wood was beside me and the woodstove in the kitchen just needed a match to get another blaze going. Anticipating a possible power-outage, I had two buckets of water in the kitchen and all the other necessities of life nearby. For a former city girl, I was doing all right. I was safe, protected and well equipped for the storm that was almost certainly on its way. Full of contentment, pleased with the solitude, I began to read again.

Out of the corner of my eye, I saw a large white shape amble into my field of vision. Ryan had re-joined the world after her post breakfast nap. She stood quietly looking out the window assessing the possibilities of what might lie out there. When she ambled over for her ears to be massaged, I was still hoping she would go back to sleep and I could read in peace. But she knew it was time for her walk and weather was irrelevant.

She loved winter. When she ran through the drifts, the snow spread out behind her in a v-shape as that deep chest and strong legs carried her with grace and power to wherever she wanted to go. She could cover miles without tiring. She was elegant but not dainty; she weighed 150 pounds and stood thirty-two inches at the shoulder.

I agreed to the walk because I knew she was missing her friend Ben who had gone into the city earlier that morning with Tom. I pulled on boots, mitts and parka. I didn't snap on the lead as I knew no one would be out on the cottage roads today. Tom and I were the only permanent residents on this side of the lake so in winter we lived in splendid isolation.

As we turned onto the road I was glad I had bundled up. The mid-December wind was biting and as it picked up strength, it lashed the upper branches of the pine trees. Snow had come early that year and then a thaw. Yesterday, freezing rain had made the roads icy so I kept to the side where the snow was crunchy and gave me some traction. Ryan of course had no problem—her legs ended in nails that could grip ice without slipping. Her normal off-lead pattern was to gallop ahead of me on the road or into the woods, come back, say hello, walk sedately for a few minutes, and then do another gallop. But today she stayed close, perhaps thinking that with Tom and Ben away she should stay close to her human who had only two legs and a useless sort of body.

We didn't go far as the walking was difficult. We turned around and as I began to pick my way through the ruts, I turned to make sure Ryan was still with me. In an instant I was flat on my back with my ankle twisted underneath. For a moment I felt nothing. Looking up through the forest canopy I saw a sky that was dark and low. Icy pellets of snow hit my nose and cheeks and then the insidious cold began seeping into my back. Reality came into focus—first pain, and then a sickening sensation of fear. I was alone, and more than half-a-mile from home. Tom would not be back until late afternoon and it was only mid-morning. There were no houses nearby and the chances of anyone finding me were non-existent. Meanwhile a blizzard was now swirling around me.

Slowly, painfully, I turned on my side trying to protect the lower part of the left leg. The ankle was not doing well. I was able to sit up but that was all I could do. During this manoeuvring, I knew Ryan was there, hovering, occasionally licking my face. I patted her and sat for a moment figuring out a strategy. I tried crawling towards the woods to find a large stick to support me but there was nothing. I was on a stretch of road where the lake was on one side and a deep gully on the other. I sat quietly for a moment getting my breath. The silence wrapped itself around me; the wind had died and the snow was thick and heavy. The sense of wanting to sink into that enveloping quietness was powerful—just to be able to stop struggling and be absorbed into the whiteness.

Then, through the silence, I heard the unmistakable and haunting howl of a wolf.

If I hadn't been in pain, I would have smiled at a reality that seemed stage-managed. The forest scene was almost too perfect. The snowy road, the winter storm, the howling wolf and a woman in distress. What a cliché. But the cliché was real and I was worried. The menace came from my fear and vulnerability. But Mother Nature was only shaking herself out. My job was to get out of the way. Ryan knew this as she gently nudged me into awareness. Her large expressive eyes held no fear, just an imperative: *Let's go.*

She stood beside me, her head turned into the wind. Suddenly she turned and butted me. I appreciated the gesture of affection but it wasn't going to help. Then she butted me again, harder this time, and leaned into me with her whole body. When I didn't react, she pulled back, looked me in the eye with an exasperated look on her face as though to say: *Pay attention.* Finally, I understood. I lifted one arm over her shoulder as she bent down, doing a four-footed curtsy, and put the other hand deep into the fur on her other shoulder. With a lot of heaving and groaning I was able to pull myself into a crouching position. She stayed perfectly still until I was standing on both feet. Then, slowly, painfully, we made our way down the hill and along the road towards home. Ryan stayed with me, never trying to hurry me, acting like a living crutch for the whole journey.

Much later, we heaved ourselves up the steps, through the door and collapsed on the kitchen floor. My arms were around Ryan's great head and my face was buried in her cold wet fur. She gave me a few perfunctory licks and then, with a great sigh, fell asleep.

Tightening my arms, I remembered all the connections that led me to Ryan: Caleb, Betty, Susan and the male-hating Cara. They had all helped to bring me to this moment with this dog.

But my boots were still on my feet, snow had melted in large pools under my legs, and my parka was unzipped but still on. As I watched the large mop of wet fur beside me, it opened a large brown eye, the head half lifted off the floor, fell back and then sleep overtook her again. I began to feel hunger and the need to attend to a throbbing ankle.

When I opened the fridge door, surveying the contents, looking to see if there was anything fit for lunch, I realized I had company. Ryan had ducked her head under my elbow and her nose was twitching. She knew that there was a meaty bone in there and she also knew that she deserved it. She was right. While she was gnawing on the bone, full of fierce satisfaction, I made a ham sandwich and carried it back to the freshly stoked fire and my waiting book. It was Alice Munro's *Lives of Girls and Women*. A fine author, but with little to say about dogs. A shame really.

Ryan died on December 21, 1999 from a deadly form of pneumonia. She suffered for thirty-six hours, stretching that long elegant neck as far as she could, trying to pull air into her lungs, unable to lie down. Tom and I spent most of one dreadful night sponging her body with cool water trying to get her raging fever down. Neither medication nor love could help. Finally, she slipped into a coma and then, that wonderful laughing spirit was gone.

Tom, Ben and Luie

In the beginning of the "dog days" at Tamarack Lake, I watched Tom work with his playful but earnest little puppy and I learned as much about Tom as I did about puppy training. Even though we were armed with all the books (we especially liked Brian Kilcommons' *Good Owners Great Dogs* and Tom's favourite, *How to Be Your Dog's Best Friend* by the Monks of New Skete.) We even had a video.

Tom read everything and then brought his own brand of loving attention to the job of training Ben. Being a much more patient person than me, he was able to repeat the same small bit of training over and over until Ben "got it". But occasionally, like most dog owners, he was ready to throttle the puppy who insisted on doing things his way. And then there was a battle of wills with Tom getting red in the face and Ben looking defiant because he could not or would not get his head around the necessity of staying where and when he was told. According to his puppy brain, that was just wrong and why couldn't Tom see that. But eventually his love for and need to please Tom won out.

They both learned the game of "two sticks" a great work out for both dog and man. Tom would throw a stick, Ben would go bounding after it, and as he headed back, Tom would throw another stick in the opposite direction. After fifteen minutes of this both of them were panting from exertion. Ben learned about the "recall" in a sneaky but fun way, and Tom lost a few pounds.

When Ben was nine months old they embarked on the first stage of Schutzhund dog training, a German sport involving obedience, protection and tracking. They went off to classes together every week and at home watched videos featuring perfectly trained dogs who went faultlessly through the complicated training. Ben would watch this for a while, excited by the barking on the screen, but after a few minutes would curl up on his bed and have a nap—either out of boredom or a sense of inferiority.

The protection segment of the training involved the dog's focused attention; he must warn the well padded "intruder", and then hold him at bay without harming, without biting. Just looking and sounding as though he might. The other dogs loved this part of the training and thought it was a great game. They were joyfully exuberant with their owners after the session was over. But not Ben. He couldn't get the hang of looking and sounding fierce. Not for a game.

I worried when Ben came back looking unhappy and exhausted. Tom thought he would eventually get the idea. We had a few words but I knew Tom was worried too. After a few weeks the instructor told Tom, as kindly as possible; that Ben was just too kind-hearted and gentle to be a successful Schutzhund dog. Tom was disappointed but I breathed a sigh of relief.

During those weeks of training Tom had met a man who also had a gentler method of training. Even though he had titled several dogs himself in Schutzhund, his methods were much different and always involved lots of treats, kindness and humour. So Tom and Hans began a routine of dog training that was much easier on Tom, Ben and me.

One winter day while working with the dogs, Tom slipped on the ice and took a hard fall. Hans came rushing over, full of concern, ran past Tom lying on the ground nursing his leg and knelt in the snow to examine Ben (who was perfectly fine). His words to Tom, which Tom never let him forget were, "You silly bugger. You could have hurt Ben!"

Ben never got a Schutzhund title but he became a well-behaved, happy and loving dog. He became a playful, nurturing big brother to our third member of the canine family and second Wolfhound, Luie (short for Hallelujah). When Luie was very young, Ben was careful with her. He would mouth her but never bite and he never got impatient, unlike Ryan who would quickly get tired of her puppy antics and stalk off to a quiet corner. But Ben never tired of her and allowed her to crawl all over him and take his bones and toys right out of his mouth.

When Luie got to be as big as he was, when she was about six months old, their favourite game was to see who could jump highest. After their leaping, they would fall back on top of one another and roll on the ground together. But one day as they fell back on one another, the buckle on Ben's collar caught on one of Luie's front teeth, the long canine just to the side. As they tried to pull apart, the collar pulled tighter as both dogs writhed in pain and in panic. Luie because her tooth was being pulled, Ben because he was choking. Tom and I were there instantly but the buckle could not be loosened. I rushed to the house to get a sharp knife, but the pressure on Ben's jugular had stopped the blood flow and he was gone before I got back.

Tom cradled Ben in his arms, tears streaming down his face. At the animal hospital the vet said it was a freak accident, but one she had seen before.

The other dogs, Ryan and Luie, were in mourning. They lay on the deck staring up the driveway for a very long time. Tom turned silent and went into his own world. I cooked, fed dogs and people. I swam in solitude a lot that summer.

One day, several weeks after Ben's death, I said to Tom, "You need your own special dog again. I have Ryan, you'll have Luie. I think she loves you more than me anyway." Tom agreed. I thought he might want to wait a bit longer and then get a German Shepherd pup. But no, he thought Luie would do just fine.

And that began Tom's love affair with Wolfhounds. While Ben was alive, Wolfhounds were pretty much my territory. Their personalities and temperament were very different from a German Shepherd's and Tom didn't know what to make of their independence and lack of unthinking devotion. But he did love their spirit, their joy in life, as well as the sheer beauty of their bodies in motion.

Luie had come to us because my friend Susan, a world-class breeder of Irish Wolfhounds, had said, "You love the breed; why not get another show quality puppy that you and Tom could show in conformation trials?" Those were just words to me. Conformation? Show puppies? Not in my universe. Tom had done some showing of German Shepherds years before my time, so he was interested. All I heard was: another puppy? *Oh boy! Count me in.*

So Hallelujah, born in May of 1996, had a great pedigree but more importantly, a sweet and loving disposition. Luckily for Tom she was also very trainable in spite of her breed's independence and annoying tendency to ask "What for?" when given a command. She and Tom became a pair and won many ribbons. She not only became a Canadian champion in the show ring but Tom managed to get her titled in the obedience ring. Quite an achievement for this hard-to-train breed. But Luie and Tom loved each other and it showed. He had a special blend of kindness and something every good dog trainer has—an expectation that of course the dog will do as she is asked. (With Wolfhounds, even with Luie, there were always a few caveats, but they were never exercised in the ring—fair is fair).

and there were more...

We were hooked on Irish Wolfhounds. Seamus and Breej joined us—
Breej from Ryan's kennel and the Dunnescroft line, Seamus from
Susan's Glenamadda line—kin to Luie.

Seamus was Tom's boy from the moment he was born on June 9,
2000. When the time came for him to be born, when his mother was
just starting labour, Susan called us and said, "You'd better hurry."
Within minutes Tom was in the car and on his way to the Glenamadda
kennels in the Caledon hills. He was there just in time for the birth
and to pick the tiny, blind ball of fluff who would become a gorgeous,
180-pound, red brindle coloured dog—according to the records, he was
officially, Glenamadda Navajo Shaman—but we called him Seamus.

Susan and Tom began showing him as soon as he was eligible for
the conformation ring. He loved it. Unlike many hounds who look on
show rings as one of the absurdities of the human condition, Seamus all
but pranced into the ring. He went through his paces like a pro. I was
always there, usually with whatever dog wasn't being shown that day.
But one day we noticed a slight hitch in his right leg. It wasn't serious,
his hips were fine and he was in good health, but regretfully, we pulled
him from the ring just shy of his championship. Conformation rules
are strict. Any hint of a behavioural or physical problem disqualifies
a dog.

But by then Tom had begun training Seamus for obedience trials.
Both of them enjoyed it much more than conformation. Seamus was
able to be "Mr. Personality" as he effortlessly performed all those well-

practiced moves. It was obvious that he loved the work and thought it was play compared to all the worried-looking border collies and the intense, no-nonsense German Shepherds. He just kept looking at Tom with his smiling brown eyes and wolfy grin. They made it look like a walk in the park on a sunny day. Watching the two of them in the ring was a joy; they were a team and they loved working together. At one show, dozens of spectators crowded around the ring where Seamus was doing his stuff. When he had done the last recall and the last sit, the entire audience burst into applause with whistles and cheers. Not a common sight at obedience trials. Seamus got his ribbon and an excellent score. Tom didn't stop beaming for days.

In his last years, Seamus did therapy work with Tom which meant visiting local hospitals and nursing homes. He brought the same vitality and discipline to the job but this time his gentleness and love of people were allowed to shine without any other requirements. He developed an instinct for knowing how to comfort the very sick and the dying. His great head would rest on the bed close to the hand of the sick person with Tom's hand lightly holding his leash. He wouldn't move a muscle until he felt the slight movement of a hand towards his head. Then slowly, carefully, he would move his head so the patient could hold on to the warmth and love that was Seamus.

The summer after Tom's death, Seamus' right leg developed a corrosive form of arthritis. We treated it and managed the pain fairly well but going up stairs became difficult, and some days even walking was painful. One night we both camped out on the front lawn because going up the few steps at the front or the back of the house was too painful. When my daughter Jennifer arrived from Vancouver, Seamus hobbled down the front steps, as close to bounding as he had come for a long time, and gave her a typical bump and grind Seamus welcome. His tail almost wagged itself into circles. With Jen's arm around him, he got back up the steps, into the hallway and collapsed. He never got up again; his legs had become paralyzed. Three days later the dreaded diagnosis of lymphoma was made and I knew that it was time to let Seamus' wonderful spirit move on.

for the love of dogs, we let them go

All of our dogs lived with us for a while, were loved extravagantly, imprinted their personalities on us and then, left us. Sometimes their going was peaceful, sometimes not. Ben's was not. He strangled on his collar which was caught and held by Luie's tooth. He was just two.

Ryan, our first Wolfhound died in December, 1999 of a vicious strain of pneumonia.. She was five.

Luie died with an apologetic look in her soft eyes after eating a work sock. She developed liver disease after Ryan died and couldn't have survived surgery. She was six.

Seamus died peacefully of lymphoma with his head on my lap. He was seven.

Oliver was an always frustrated Australian Shepherd who couldn't understand why Wolfhounds refused to be herded. He developed cancer and died a few weeks after Seamus. He was ten.

Breej was the most beautiful and smartest of them all. She was the last Wolfhound and was with me for almost two years after Seamus and Oliver died. She developed an inoperable tumour in her shoulder. Again, the decision was made to let her go rather than spend her last days filled with pain. She was eight.

Each one of those deaths cloaked the house in dreadful silence and grief. And each time, someone would say, almost accusingly, why must you have dogs—especially such a short lived breed. I never did have an answer, probably because I can't, on some level, comprehend the question. To answer it properly, one would have to develop not only a philosophy of dogs, but an explanation of loving detachment and the difficult concept of surrender. Of letting go. Of loving without any expectations. Of how joy, even if it is only rented, makes future pain bearable. And of how grief can open, not close a human heart.

Perhaps the oddest expression of how grief seeps into consciousness happened just after Seamus died. The vet had come to the house and while I held Seamus, talked and sang to him, she administered the needle that he didn't see coming and didn't feel. Then Jennifer, my son John and I kissed him good-bye and he was taken away by the vet and her assistant.

The three of us stayed sitting on the hardwood floor for a few minutes. I watched the sun slanting into the room. I remembered holding Seamus while saying, "Go, be with Tom." And then, how his head lifted for a moment as he gazed out the open doorway. And how, even though my tears were turning into sobs, I thought, *I must be making this up. Next I'll be hearing a choir of angels and the Virgin Mary telling me to 'Weep not'.*

The mind makes strange end-runs when emotions are in full flood. Grief has many faces. Some of them wildly beautiful. That day we danced them. In sorrow, in remembrance and in joy.

Sitting on the floor, all I could feel was a blank and awful emptiness. Without thinking, I moved to a stack of CDs and pushed one into the player. I have no idea why I picked the sound track album for the movie *The Big Chill,* but in a moment the opening notes of *I Heard it Through the Grapevine* filled the room. Again without thinking, I stood up and started to move in a slow shuffling dance. Jennifer and John joined me and we danced for Seamus.

the calendar

Memory sometimes picks me up by the scruff of the neck and shakes me until my teeth rattle. One day, early in November, I got a telephone call. The pleasant sounding woman confirmed my name and then said, "I have a Brown Trout calendar for you."

"There must be some mistake. I didn't order a calendar."

"I know. But Mark Rayburn, the dog photographer, is a friend and has left one here for you. He took pictures of your dogs for the Irish Wolfhound calendar."

For a moment I felt that I was either stupid or in a time warp. "Are you sure there is no mistake? Those pictures were taken in the fall of 2001 for the 2002 calendar. This is eight years later!"

The woman at the pet store was patient, but all she knew was that she had a big glossy calendar with my name on it. She told me where the store was located and said that I could pick it up anytime. I thanked her and put the phone down with a thud. My heart was beating fast, but I ignored it, thinking, *I've seen those pictures dozens of times, this is no big deal.* So I got on with whatever life, the universe and I had decided to do that day.

Four months later, after several false starts, many days of saying how I must get to Peterborough, a drive of about ninety minutes, I still hadn't collected the calendar. But then the day came. My friend Dorothy suggested a trip to the Costco store in Peterborough—time to stock up on a few household needs and have lunch at St. Veronus. This was a very tempting offer. I could live without stocking up on toilet paper and canned tuna, but St. Veronus, originally owned by Trappist monks and providing delectable European food, was my favourite restaurant. Great beer too.

So that Wednesday morning, we left Haliburton with my nonchalant remark, "There's a pet store near the restaurant and I'd like to pick up a calendar." Of course she wondered why I was picking up a calendar in March so I explained how eight years ago, a photographer had contacted Tom and I wanting to take pictures of our two Wolfhounds, Seamus and Breej. If all went well, they might be used in a forthcoming calendar. So off we had gone for a photo shoot in a lovely Peterborough park. It was a fun if frustrating experience.

The dogs were still very young and much more interested in running than posing for pretty pictures. Seamus eventually decided that he would do his best to look handsome for the nice man who had cookies in his pocket, but Breej, like her forbear Ryan, had a mind of her own and it didn't include standing nicely—cookies or no cookies. So when we saw the proofs, there were several excellent shots of Seamus, one fairly good one of the two of them and none of "Herself". When the calendar came out a few months later, there were two months that were graced by Seamus' picture including the cover shot. Breej didn't make it as a calendar girl but I doubt that she was concerned. A picture of Seamus turned up, surprisingly, in later years—2003 and 2004, then nothing more.

That day in Peterborough, shopping and lunch over, it was with anticipation, and a bit of trepidation, that I picked up the calendar. Standing in that rather small, trendy, boutique-style pet store on the main street of the small Ontario city of Peterborough, I noticed with surprise that my hands were trembling. Just a bit. I told myself that the emotion was understandable. Tom and I had trained, lived with and loved those animals for many years. And this was like a ghostly hand from the past reaching out to me. But I had mourned their deaths. Breej had died two years ago this month and Seamus the year after

Tom's death. One of the pictures Mark had taken of them was on my windowsill. This was not a new grief.

But the tears pricking the back of my eyelids were for the monstrous pain of loss, for all the deaths, the losses and the wrenching regrets. Grief is a country I am familiar with. I know its hills and valleys, its bogs and its deserts. That pricking of tears was not unfamiliar. Just surprising.

So as I walked back to the car, clutching the shrink-wrapped package, I thought: *What is this about?* But then another, different brain responded: *What a stupid question. You expect the grieving to have an end? You think you can wrap it up and tuck it away like a worn-out sweater?*

I opened the car door and sat in stillness for a moment. Then the giant wheel of consciousness clicked into the next slot—the one that holds the place where sadness and love and grief live. Grief that someone, some creature, some place, is gone, and so the soul yearns. But the yearning is also a gift. A remembrance of joy and laughter and love. The richness of life includes grief and I will never be allowed to forget that. I blinked back the tears and turned to my friend. "Let's go. I'll show you the calendar when we stop for coffee."

Later, I explained to Dorothy, "Breej didn't make it into the calendar, she was way too silly that day." But Seamus was "Mr. May 2010", a headshot with his bright, deep amber eyes looking right at the camera and his cowlicks sticking straight up, as always. As "Mr. August", he was caught standing in front of an old stone wall, the soft golden colour of the stones matching his coat.

I wanted to hug him through the calendar, through the years, through the tears, but when you allow yourself to be owned by dogs, sadness is part of the deal.

Part Four
Memories and Dreams

rites of spring

Life at the cottage wasn't entirely about dogs even though they seemed to dominate those years. Sometimes it was about water.

I have heard people say, in the face of whatever calamity that might befall them, "I'm not worried. The universe (substitute God, Allah, or Spirit as needed) will take care of me!"

There are many possible responses to this statement but I usually try to avoid them for the sake of good manners and peace in the world. In my experience, what the universe provides may or may not be what you had in mind. And it would be extremely unwise to trust that the mind of the universe is running on the same track as yours.

Today, much against my wishes, the universe is sending rain. A lot of rain. Normally that would be fine and I would be grateful because it isn't white and I don't have to shovel it. But the back yard, the front yard and everything in between is still covered with mounds, mountains in fact, of leftover melting snow. And that of course is a very mixed blessing. Too much melting too quickly might result in the universe providing me with a wet basement. Floating water-logged books, cushions, assorted debris and the possibility of a drowned mouse or two does not fill me with gratitude to the above-mentioned universe. I'm not angry or feeling victimized. The Universe, or God, or Spirit is simply going about Her business, trying to keep everything in balance, despite our destructive interference, and doesn't particularly care about water-logged books or dead mice. Unfortunately, I do.

As Bertrand Russell said, it would behoove the chicken, who watched the farmer come out with food every morning but one day came out with an axe instead, to have a more comprehensive view of the universe. So here I am, peering out the window, checking the floor of the basement periodically and trying not to have the naiveté of the chicken, trying to think comprehensively, trying to think of options. Last night was pretty restless. So I must admit, as at other times of duress, I sent a message to Tom. *I know you can't just pull on a pair of rubber boots and help if we do get a flood, but could you please use whatever influence you might have to keep the melting at a manageable rate? Thank you very much.*

I'm afraid I do send out messages like that; not very often, but when things, as things do, take off in unmanageable directions, I do ask for help.

A few years ago we worked in shifts for a week trying to keep water out of the basement. For many days we had a pump and a wet vacuum going around the clock. That was the year the ground froze weeks before the snow came so when it melted in the spring, a solid ice pack formed over the ground and the water had no place to go. We went out with shovels and pickaxes making miniature ditches in the ice and snow so that the melting snow would be diverted away from the house. Not a time I remember with a lot of fondness but we were pretty magnificent, if I do say so—especially Tom.

So in the midst of today's scariness, I'm remembering other situations with water and I am missing both his calmness and his big shoulders. We were a good team although sometimes there were glitches—glitches that often sounded like two kids saying: "You're not the boss of me!" and "You're not the boss of me either!" Tom always hated being told what to do. Unfortunately, under stress, I tend to get a bit bossy. So, sometimes we would stare at each other with red faces and then stalk away.

One day, when we were still living at the cottage on Tamarack Lake, I had stalked all the way down to the dock, jumped in and stayed there until the water cooled me off. It took most of the afternoon. It was never all beer and skittles between us but whenever we had to figure out how to cope with something we did it together.

The first summer we bought the cottage was also when we had our first water situation. We had gone to bed early and fell sound asleep after a hard day of trying out the new hammock and floating around on the lake in inner tubes. Sometime after midnight we both sat bolt up in bed. There had been a tremendous clap of thunder, and then, another more frightening noise; the sound of rushing water. We ran to the front of the cottage and looked down at a lake lapping benignly on the sand beach even though the rain was slanting down like a solid sheet of water. Then we hurried around to the back door. Looking up the hill behind the cottage we saw another wall of water. But this one was a waterfall, dredging the soil and carrying it toward the cottage.

Tom pulled on his jeans and was out the door. I rushed out in a t-shirt and running shoes. We quickly found shovels and hoes, newly purchased for the freshly planted vegetable garden that was now heading for the lake. We got to work digging trenches and miniature dikes. Eventually we were able to change the direction of the water. When we finally stopped, Tom's hair was plastered to his forehead and his jeans were sagging well below his belly. My t-shirt felt like a second skin, my running shoes felt like they weighed ten pounds, and I was suddenly conscious that I had forgotten to pull on pants.

But we felt absolutely wonderful. We looked at the result of our hard work and felt like the engineers who built the Aswan Dam.

So today, keeping an eye on the basement, watching the water rush down the driveway, hoping it doesn't wash out the sides again as it did that year of the flood, I think of Tom, in his yellow rain jacket and shovel, doing the best he could to keep us safe.

I also know that very soon we will have our usual spring—often like time-lapse photography where you see a flower bud opening slowly and miraculously into full bloom in a matter of seconds. That is the way spring is up here. One day the remnants of a dirty snow blanket are still covering the garden. The next day green shoots are poking up out of bare earth. And a few days after that, there are crocuses blooming all over the lawn. It is so beautiful that you forget about the water and the mud.

Today, my rubber boots with their eye-catching and fashionable red stripe are waiting for me by the back door. But I'm remembering daffodils, tulips and Tom.

life in a garden

August 25, 2005

Tom discovered hand drumming late in life. Three months ago he was stricken with a stroke as he started a new rhythm on his beloved djembe. The world lost a good man and a passionate, if flawed, drummer. I miss the drumming, his wonderful grin, his stories from all the corners of his vastly interesting life, and his quick concern for those he loved.

But I also miss that amazing upper body strength that allowed him to wheel a load of manure into my garden, dump it and spread it without even raising a sweat. Yes, I miss my assistant (if not always constant) gardener.

And so does the garden. It has been shamefully neglected.

Now it is August, and I am looking at a garden choked with weeds. A few spindly tomato plants have persevered and produced some hard, green tomatoes. Many of the flowers, desperately seeking sunshine and nutrients, have not quite given up the battle with the weeds. But some have of course. They have coughed once, delicately, and expired. It was just all too much for them. But the mallows, the daylilies, the daisies and the yarrow are standing tall, proliferating, and going *mano a mano* with the weeds.

The burrs and brambles are poking through the fences and in other hidden places. These must be attended to very soon. Burrs tend to have a magnetic attraction for dogs' muzzles and between the pads on their paws; it is a painful, tedious process to remove them. It is these dreadful plants, innocuous and hidden for many weeks, which suddenly throw off their shy, retiring ways and become zealots dedicated to taking over the earth. I digress. I allow these pusillanimous plants to enrage me. Right now the garden seems to be defeating me. It certainly is defeating my carefully made plans. Some days, I'd like to rent a guy with a load of green cement. But instead, I will do what absolutely must be done and the rest will be ignored. The weeds will set seed, multiply and proliferate. They will make their mad plans. But I will make sure that the burrs are gone. If I am lucky, there will be tomatoes for salads and enough basil for pesto.

August 28, 2005

I visited my garden again today. This time the joyously proliferating weeds no longer seemed to be looming minions of evil. In spite of my lethargy and disinterest in the garden, I found myself making small pathways through the weeds. I had thought the nasturtiums had disappeared in the chaos of crabgrass, no-name weeds and the rogue rose canes which were popping up all over the garden. Yet, there they were; enough yellow, orange and red blooms to fill the deep blue jug with the chipped rim that I keep just to show off their brilliance. It would look well on the kitchen windowsill.

But the garden was not finished surprising me. Bending over, I saw tiny broccoli florets in among the yellow spires of plants gone to seed. I picked a handful. Then more surprises! A few tiny cherry tomatoes bursting off the vine, a few oversized green onions, and finally, a large, perfectly round scarlet tomato, still warm from the sun. I filled the front of my t-shirt with what seemed to be my ill-gotten gains. While opening the garden gate, I looked around at this neglected garden. It was lush and busy. This amazing piece of earth was still working away and its generosity astounded me.

Next January the wonderful, overblown seed catalogues will arrive with their siren call to buy more seeds, more plants, more joy. There will be pages and pages of glowing red tomatoes, broccoli and beans so green it would make an Irishman blush. And there will be flowers: shy but heartfelt primroses peeking from their canopy of leaves, tall blowsy zinnias so bright they seem to be dripping with fresh paint, glorious tea roses tempting me to defy Haliburton's climate just one more time.

Once again, I shall be entranced and I shall put my faith in the snake oil salesmen who write these catalogues. Once again, I shall put my faith in the totally unfounded belief that I can make a garden. Tom will not be around to do all the "gardener's assistant" jobs; although there will be a ghostly presence checking to make sure that the tomatoes are well staked and the peas have a place to climb. So I must attend to those things as well as to the matter of the manure. And once again, there will be a garden.

life in a garden: part two

September 9, 2006

As the light faded in the garden tonight, I was sitting, or actually squatting on my haunches, amidst the floppy onion stalks and the too-bushy tomato plants. This garden would be unacceptable not only to a horticultural society, but to anyone who has ever plunked a seed in the ground and hoped for the best. In recent years, I had been setting my standards somewhat lower and had planted fewer rows of vegetables, but this garden was sub-standard even for me.

From my vantage point close to the ground, I could see that weeds vastly outnumbered the brave vegetables and flowers. Some of them had come up from seeds and were still struggling with the vicissitudes of life. Others had been bought at a nursery and carefully placed in the ground with the appropriate manure, organic add-ins to make them strong and prolific, and a large dose of misplaced hope. A little later, compost had been harvested and applied. Knowing that roses loved the potassium in bananas, I had shredded many of them and served them up as a special delectable treat. I must say the roses have been beautiful this year. But now they were moping.

Last year I had given over one of the beds to perennial flowers; ones that would be undemanding and look after themselves as they multiplied. They did. But unfortunately the weeds were better at it. They obviously had no truck with the perennials' methods of family planning.

Looking up, I noticed that the sun was low in the sky. September brings an early sunset so by seven o'clock the light is gentler and softer and seems to encourage each plant to glow from the inside out. As I gazed at this neglected garden, each plant and flower and weed, every living thing for as far as I could see, was glowing and glorious. I sank back even further on my heels until my bottom was actually sitting on the soft earth. My gratitude at being a witness to this beauty was overwhelming—for a moment.

But then the softness of reverie passed. I realized that I had to get up from this awkward position and it was not going to be easy. It was going to be damn difficult. I felt locked in position, as though I had grown roots into the ground, like one of the onions. This painful awkwardness was a fairly new reality for me. My knees, hips, back and shoulders were no longer doing what they were supposed to do. Getting up and down was not only an unlovely exercise in callisthenics, it was also painful. And that was why the weeds had taken over. They knew they were safe.

Under Tom's watchful eye, weeding was done fairly regularly, at least until mid-summer. The grassy pathways between the raised vegetable plots were kept reasonably neat. Tom objected to my flinging weedy debris onto those pathways, but I usually ignored him, feeling that my sense of righteousness at weeding should not be sullied by such carping.

In winter, there was satisfaction in perusing those alluring seed catalogues, planning what would go where, turning the soil in May, fertilizing with a careful mixture of homemade compost, manure, wood ashes and a bit of lime. Finally, we would settle the seeds and the tiny plants in the ground, always with a hope and a prayer. We would spend long back-breaking and knee-destroying hours out there. Tom would dig holes, move compost and manure around and later, at the end of the day, would holler at me to come in before I hurt myself. Sometimes I listened, sometimes not, but always I heard the concern.

By early July we were eating the first tender leaves of lettuce and the sugar snap peas (which sometimes made it as far as the kitchen). As the heat of July descended, we watched the blossoms on the tomato plants turn from yellow flowers into tiny green spheres. The beans were also setting flowers and the broccoli was busy growing its own tight little green heads. The garden was a lush and busy place.

Eventually, August's heat drained our energy as it energized the plants. The weeds, also energized, fought the vegetables for living space. But in spite of these territorial wars, most things in the garden thrived. We even enjoyed the shifting balance of power as insects, varmints and weeds became more insistent and more prolific. Because there was always enough to go around.

But now it is the end of the second summer of neglect. Next year there will be tables: tables holding big pots of tomatoes, beans, cucumbers and onions. There will be more tables with pots of herbs: dill, parsley, sage, rosemary and thyme. Cilantro might have a big pot all to itself. Of course there will be all the homely annuals that I love: pansies, marigolds, daisies, cosmos and zinnias. And I could never forget the nasturtiums, both climbing and upright, and maybe even a new rose.

The reverie in the garden is helping me to let go. To let go of the joy of many years of digging in the dirt, coaxing things to grow, trying for a balance that never quite happened—a balance between my grandiose plans and nature's own grand profligacy.

That weed-filled garden, glowing with life and sunlight was nature at her best—chuckling at my distress, but understanding it. She was laughing with a great cosmic delight, tempered with compassion, for mortal wrong-headedness.

September 5, 2007

Tomatoes, beans, lettuce and herbs were planted in pots and baskets this year, but with the same careful attention to their living arrangements as in other years. I have feasted on luscious tomatoes, but then so have the squirrels and chipmunks. In fact this year the numbers of these creatures has greatly increased. I don't mind sharing the bounty of the garden (or the pots) but when it becomes a battle for each tomato, then those cute bushy-tailed pests with the bright eyes are just rodents, rats with designer tails. Just as the tomatoes begin to turn from pale green to pink they disappear. Some of these bushy-tailed rats are even defying me by nibbling on their stolen lunches right in front of me. Luckily, they left me a few and since they don't seem to be fond of greens, salads aren't entirely missing from my diet.

The former vegetable garden is now totally out of control. The militant weeds have now colonized that once thriving plot of summer vegetables and are shamelessly enjoying the anarchy of uninhibited nature. It does have its own beauty, I admit that, but it is a beauty that doesn't belong in a garden. I suppose that is the issue; I don't have a "garden" anymore. I have a weed bed.

Perhaps someday, someone else will decide to make a garden here. She will dig up the weeds; turn the soil and plant rows of broccoli, lettuce, beans, tomatoes and whatever else she might want to grow. And once again the weeds will be given a run for their money.

Sometimes this process of constant change makes me weep. I want to keep things the same; I don't want to give up one thing for another when what I must give up is so astoundingly precious. Yet other times, in more complacent moods, it is easier to let go, to relish the present moment and anticipate, with serenity, the next page. Because there always is a next page, and I cannot be mindful of its wonders and challenges if I cling to the beauty that was.

Tomorrow or next week I might truly understand and appreciate that ancient wisdom. But today I am grieving. And remembering.

tea and cookies

Some of the things consciousness chooses to remember can be odd.

Tom loved Fig Newton cookies and I didn't. A fairly trivial fact but it had repercussions. He liked to sit down with a nice cup of tea with a plate of Fig Newtons and feel instantly comforted. I on the other hand, had little use for tea (except on rare occasions) and even less use for Fig Newtons. To me, they were not really cookies. With their soft mealiness, they tasted of nothing and the filling, made up of sweetened fig puree, had a puzzling aftertaste.

Even though I mostly held my peace about their basic unattractiveness, maybe I could have learned to like them. Or even pretended to find something worthwhile in them.

But I didn't. And now I'm sorry. It wouldn't have cost much. He would have been happy; I would have felt like a loving wife.

But that would have been some other couple.

Tom's table

I heard the front door open and a moment later Tom appeared in the doorway of our kitchen. The longer I stared at his face, the more distinctly I saw cat whiskers and a few glistening drops of cream. Staring at him, trying for cool nonchalance I said, "Hi."

The whiskers twitched wickedly but then Tom's face swam into focus. No cream, no whiskers, just a smile that overflowed into his blue eyes. "I made you something," he said.

Tom had just completed his first woodworking course at night school.

"What is it?" I asked, feeling on the verge of hysterical and inappropriate laughter. I felt like a Mom whose child just came home from his first day at kindergarten brandishing a magnificent piece of art work which must instantly be put on the fridge anchored by a smiley face magnet.

I mentally shook myself and we walked out to the car. He opened the trunk and carefully took out the first piece of furniture he had ever made, a small bedside table. After examining it and making heartfelt sounds of appreciation, I got down on my hands and knees and took another look. My knowledge of carpentry was less than nil but I realized that it was truly a Tom table. If one nail would hold the leg to a crosspiece, then two or even three would be better. The bottom shelf was not perfectly aligned with the top one. But it was a stable, clunky little table and we both loved it. It was the kind of table that could be relied on to hold an enormous load of books without buckling. I knew that a little bit of oil and hand rubbing would bring out the grain of the wood.

Tom never advanced to more complicated items of furniture. But he made a large table in the laundry room so we could fold clothes. He made a similar one in the workshop for potting plants and holding all the garden apparatus. Neither of them ever buckled or tipped. They safely held the clutter of life without falling down. And they reminded me of something Thomas Merton said: "The peculiar grace of a Shaker chair is due to the fact that it was made by someone capable of believing that an angel might come and sit on it."

Tom never attempted a chair, but a house angel could happily fold clothes or pot plants on one of Tom's tables.

Not all of Tom's projects had such a benign afterlife. There was for example, the case of the low stone wall behind the tiny pond in the garden. When I came home from work one hot summer day it became obvious that Tom had laboured a good part of that day lugging large rocks from one part of the yard to another. That made me nervous and a little angry that he had pushed himself so hard. But since his upper body was strong and muscular, he enjoyed giving himself that kind of workout. Age, blood pressure and nagging wives be damned.

So I held back on my worried crankiness and gazed at the wall. I was about to admire his work when I noticed a rock that seemed misplaced. Just a small one but it wasn't quite right. So I took off my shoes, removed my skirt and waded into the pond to fix it. I found another smaller rock that needed to be re-positioned, just so. Then another. I glanced over at Tom. I saw storm clouds building.

"What are you doing?"

"Just moving a couple of rocks," I said.

"Why can't you just leave things alone?" he said, sitting down heavily.

So there it was. The submerged mountain range of resentment that triggered more marital arguments and tight-lipped discussions than anything else. Tom and I could sail through floods, financial disasters, issues over his kid versus my kid and remain friends. But my need to find a better way, another way, could bring us to the brink of war.

Being deep in a relationship means letting go of our usual boundaries and defences. Sometimes that means letting loose the shadow. And when the shadows of a loving couple confront each other, in unblinking and perhaps unconscious hostility, there is always war.

Usually we tiptoed away from that brink of war, but not always. Those were the times when we discovered what marriage was all about. Those were the hard patches, where humour and love and compassion got swept away in a torrent of anger and frustration and bruised ego. And there wasn't always a happy ending, or any ending. Just an exhausted need to go on. Regardless. And so we did.

Tom's mystical relationship to money

I have always had an odd and conflicted relationship with money. At least I thought it was odd until I met Tom's. Throughout our marriage, Tom and I rarely discussed money except in a roundabout, vague sort of way. As in:

Tom: "Where should we go this year for our holiday?"

Pat: "We've had a lot of expenses this year, and the cottage needs a new roof." But before I had even finished the sentence, Tom would have disappeared around a corner or into a book.

Tom's first wife Anne always took care of everything financial. He had never written a cheque until she went to India for a month and she gave him a crash course in household finance before leaving. Little of it stuck. He loved shopping and buying things or better yet, having me buy things for myself. He was a classic "enabler". I became cautious about saying how much I liked something because his response was always, "Well, you should get it!" And that for him was that. I, too, often, would happily agree.

Sometimes I was careless about the small things. Tom was extravagant with the larger items, like power tools, lawnmowers, and snowblowers. Or a pair of ridiculously expensive, but very beautiful, leather chairs just at the time when the deck needed replacing and an expensive vet bill was looming. Compared to Tom I was almost sensible about money. His was an attitude unworldly in scope. He didn't have a relationship with money; he just expected that it would be there when he needed it. And it always was. Our financial position was never particularly serene, but on the other hand we never fell into the chaos of total disaster either.

Tom's sense of being intimately connected to the wholeness and complexity of a generous universe was his defining quality. He felt that he was connected to this generosity, and regardless of whether we were rich or poor, it was part of the mystery we were born into. Part of a changing evolving world where everything happened for a reason but it was a waste of time and energy to try to understand that meaning. Just accept that a new snowblower is a magnificent gift and be happy.

Adjusting to that view of reality was ridiculously easy.

Part Five
Grief and God

you don't cry first

The crying didn't come first. Before the crying came the scream, not a wail of loss or choking sobs. Those came later.

First came shock: this body lying on the hospital bed will never get up, never speak, never laugh, and never hold me. And that can't be born. So an enveloping, obliterating coldness takes over that shuts out the world.

Yet a day came when I knew that I could write about all of this. Not as a how-to manual for widows. I looked at a few of those and gritted my teeth. Everyone expresses grief differently and copes with the fall-out of death differently. Trying to tease out the universal strands of this process and how they are born is presumptuous or just beyond my skill.

But I believe that an enormous part of our defining humanity is a need to communicate, to bear witness to our most profound experiences. If I were to write about what I have experienced, then I believe that somewhere, sitting in a quiet pool of light, would be a reader who imagines or remembers the pain and the joy that are on the pages of a book. And out of the many acts of writing and reading comes a circle of human beings: yearning, weeping, laughing and being absorbed in the experience of being human, of not being alone.

When we speak, or read or listen to the mystery, the grief, the joy and the wonder of our lives, we lift that claustrophobic veil that separates us from the rest of the world. Responding to the stories and musings that someone puts on a page is part of the glue that holds the world together.

I knew that by writing my story I was knitting myself into the circle in a new way; that I would contribute to the membrane that holds us together as we sit under our pools of light.

In the beginning there was a plodding, teeth gritting dreariness in putting one foot in front of the other; a sense that this lack of joy would never end. But a day came when there was a shift. There was no moment of epiphany when I felt reborn. But life started stitching itself together again, and I began the long, frustrating, often reluctant journey into exploring the ground of the sacred. A ground that I understood no more than I ever did, but a tentative belief was blooming that was more hopeful Buddhist prayer flag than dogma. Whatever it was, it helped me to hold the world together. This tentative belief demanded few rituals of me except the need, on occasion, to be perfectly still. To breathe, to be exquisitely aware of the breath and to surrender to the next moment. I discovered how difficult it is to do nothing much. But space was cleared and a connection confirmed. The lines were opened.

Of course the flat-footed plodding self, the one who was too frightened to believe in the sacred because it might just be a foolish and cowardly denial of death, asserted her shrill cry of intellectual snobbery. But I ignored her more often than not. I was unmoved by her sneers that I was surrendering to fear of death, to that dreadful need to persist in being, to survive the grave. *To know that Tom is safe.*

Grief brought me to a place where there was no room for the trivial. No appetite for intellectual jousting or theological arguments. Although that did come back; one can't transcend all one's pleasures. But the grounding, and at the same time, ephemeral sense of existing in a multitude of dimensions has never left me. I am reasonably, perhaps unreasonably, sure it never will, in spite of my inner demons.

Yet I don't always want to hear about the blissful state of oceanic oneness. Yes, yes I say impatiently, I'm sure that state will come. Someday. Afterwards. If I play my cards right and don't make any pacts with the devil. But I want to know more about the *before,* the back-story to enlightenment, about the struggle, about how it felt getting there.

I also wanted to know how many frogs in the pond I must count, how much and what kind of meditation I must do, how many books, how many teachers before I get there—pre-supposing there was a there to get to.

I am told that there is a proverbial ladder with, I assume, proverbial rungs up which I must climb. But I discovered that this ladder is like the Cheshire cat's grin. Just when you get close, it fades away. So, no ladder, no rungs. Just the void, and my confusion; my struggle with how to live. Sometimes, when my heart settled into its own silence, there was an overwhelming peace. And an enfolding presence filled with compassion and memories.

Tom's death broke the dam that blocked my ability to see myself as a spiritual being and to see the inter-connectedness of the seen and the unseen. I was able to feel Tom around me, not just think about him. He became not a guide or a teacher, but the big guy sitting in the bleachers cheering me on.

The Tom stories were joyful and were usually written quickly and easily; he sat on my shoulder as I wrote about him. The other part of this story is the description of the interior struggle, the one most of us confront, often at 3:00 a.m., the one that involves God, The Great Spirit, Yahweh, The Divine Spirit, The Great Mother, or The Ultimate Ground of Being and where we stand in relation to all of that. That struggle might bring me to thoughts of transformation or frustration, but it also reminds me of a pot of geraniums falling to the ground and the promise contained in that shared moment of grace.

Alice ages

Once there was a woman who, in a moment of profound surprise, realized that she had reached the age of sixty-eight and that she had profound doubts about Wonderland.

Just yesterday she had been a child gathering her books for school. And then, a moment after that, a young wife and mother, one arm holding a nursing baby, the other the philosophy of Hegel.

And then, more pages turned, as she struggled with single parenthood and the quest for paid work that didn't make her nauseous. She was mired in relationships that crashed or were cancelled for lack of interest. Finally, she found work that was almost right and a relationship full of love and laughter. Yesterdays were past and the future slyly smiled its hidden wisdom.

Now, there is a woman, a little used up, a little tired. The words "Now what?" hold some fear and a bit of resignation. She knows, this woman who is not ancient but long past nubile, that no child leaves the womb with a sealed envelope, an owner's manual, full of careful instructions for every crisis and every turning point. But surely, she thinks, somewhere, imprinted on her soul like a laundry stamp, there must be a mission statement, written in code of course and difficult to decipher. But the stamp remains a mystery to her. Perhaps she lost her decoding ring during one of the periods when life turned her upside down and shook her. But time is running out.

So she has no instruction on how grief must be experienced. There is no template on which to lay her experience and no consoling words to pull around herself, like a shroud.

She has discovered that when a grievous loss is endured, the definition of sanity changes. Her life becomes a constant recalibration of those codes she built her life on. The ones by which she judged reality. There are no: *This is how it is and always will be forever and ever.* It is just: *This is the way it is today, this is where my energy must go. Here is where my compassion must reach. This is now. This is today and I am here.*

Sanity, like time, expands and contracts, following a rhythm that is and is not our own. We reach for control and almost grasp it. Then, with a rogue key stroke, our disciplined, adult decisions about how life is supposed to be are clicked into the delete file. And once again we are confronted by a blank page. Or, we stare at a page that is covered with hieroglyphics, wishing we had a decoding ring. Like Alice, wishing she could find her way back to Wonderland..

The Labyrinth

The curving path has a tide that pulls
the pilgrim along the way.
But the current is subtle.
It never sweeps me forward
with no regard
for the walker's pace
or state of grace.
It is the harmony of life itself
that pulls me on.

moving through grief: the beginning

Saturday, May 14, 2005

On Thursday, April 28, ten minutes into our first drum circle at the Lounge Café, Tom started dropping things. After the third time, I knew he was in trouble. I looked at his face, and his mouth was drooping badly to the left. Mark helped me get him to the car. Fay followed behind and it was the longest, fastest drive I have ever done.

Tom lived for another horrifying five days. He died at 12:30 p.m. on Tuesday May 3rd as Beth sang a lullaby.

My children and my friends have supported me physically, emotionally and spiritually.

The funeral was a celebration of Tom's life: there was drumming, an honour guard of therapy dogs, singing, storytelling and eulogies. Someone said it was the best funeral they had ever been to. Tom would have been pleased.

But now I am alone and I don't know how to bear it.

The layers of my soul
have peeled to the centre.
But maybe there is no centre.
Or it is slumbering
In some abysmal place
Far from my reach and care.

Sunday, May 15

Sometimes the stillness needs to be found and endured. But I can only stand it for a few moments at a time. Then I must find something to be busy with until that stops working too. I pick up a book and put it down. I turn on the television and turn it off. I open the fridge and close it. I try to pray, or to meditate. There is no relief. Anywhere. I feel abandoned. There is only the awfulness.

Highway 35

Tom, I carried your ashes
to the tiny plot under the pines, near the lake,
under the bluest sky that ever was.

We drove north on Highway 35.
past the cottages, and the lakes and the rock cuts.
past the ordinary people in their ordinary cars.

I envied their innocence.
I foolishly thought,
how lucky you are,
all you ordinary people in your ordinary cars,
carrying burdens like
swimsuits and kayaks,
potato chips and life jackets.

I've forgotten how that is.
I'm like the robin. The one on my front lawn early today.
The one who lifted one foot and put it down. With such care. Then
the other.
Her head swivelled and bobbed
testing the wind, uncertain,
Anxious, wanting to be safe.

Just so, I nurtured a fearful grief and watched.
Uncertain how to be.

My hands grasped the edge of the box.
It held all there was of Tom.

Or so I thought.

For a moment, the box, heavier than one might think,
(Though who the hell imagines what ashes in a box would weigh!)
made me shift a little in the seat.
The box on my lap dug into my thighs.
I jiggled it, just a bit. Northwards.

Then I heard a voice.
Insistent, calm.
I waited. Eager for enlightenment.
But it was just that familiar voice
letting me know all was well. Including the jiggling.
And once more
I heard the laughter
that changes a world.

Saturday, May 21

The awfulness is changing shape over the days and weeks. Sometimes cradling the loss and the despair allows some softness to creep in. Perhaps I'm learning to hold the awfulness with a lighter touch and with a sense that Tom's arms are holding me.

And then, finally, I can plant a few flowers, hear the birds around me and do the dishes.

Sunday, May 22
5:00 A.M.

Blue skies behind pale clouds
Birdsong ripples the silence
Peace enfolding.

Grey skies behind no clouds
Raindrops rape the garden.
Violence hovers here

No sky behind no clouds
Flowers burst into life.
Life and death again.

Saturday, June 4

Tom has been gone for a month and I am trying very hard to be with what others have called a process, to let it flow through me, to be breathed by it. But since I am an imperfect being, the need to control and to program my grief, as well as my life, is still strong

I think about the tricks consciousness can play. The frustration of staring at one of those figure-ground puzzles for example, knowing that it is possible for them to reverse themselves, for the figure to become the ground and the ground the figure. But my mind stubbornly refuses to see anything differently from what so obviously is. How silly, the mind says, *To think that what is, could be what isn't.* That's crazy-making and maybe even immoral.

So here is this priggish little mind, piously contemplating its own navel and stuck in its own process of "thinking" through its grief. It gives itself jobs; it tells stories to itself and it has wallpapered itself with timetables and to-do lists. It has little talks with itself. It would be nice to be able to say *How nice!* to my mind and to let it go. But no, that doesn't work. Give the mind an inch and it wants to spin out the story of the universe. And it never, ever, stops watching itself.

But this sometimes quite wonderful mind is only doing its job. It is supposed to think and plan and worry. It would feel like a dead-beat mind if it didn't do that. And I would never remember the names of my children.

Sometimes, after no particular effort on my part, a shift happens. That apparently implacable ground leaps into being as figure, and what had been figure, fades into ground. Then, for a few moments or a few hours, there is peace. My mind forgets that it has to make lists, forgets its sorrow, its obsession with what was, and moves into silence.

Sunday, August 15

It is now fifteen weeks. Time has such an odd way of speeding up and slowing down. Sometimes I feel Tom left just this morning. Maybe to go into town to buy bread, and will be back in a minute or so. Other times it feels that I have lived a lifetime since he died.

Today I am remembering drumming and gardening. He was a passionate drummer. Since I wasn't much of a drummer, it was the garden (and the dogs of course) that we both loved—sometimes absent-mindedly, but always with a passionate belief that this year it would be wonderful.

the Gayatri

One day, soon after Tom's funeral, I sat on my front porch, mug of tea in hand, and felt the ropes holding my sanity in place start to loosen. I carefully set the mug on the side table. I needed both hands to hold on to the plastic arms of the lawn chair. I sat up straight and pressed both feet firmly into the solid wood deck beneath them.

It was almost sunset and the strong rays of the sun streamed through the trees at eye level, piercing the leafy shadows with lasers. I heard the birds calling their goodbyes to the day. I was aware of the two Wolfhounds, Breej and Seamus, lying down with their heads pressed against the screen door, watching.

With all my might I held on to that awareness and those real sensations because I could feel control dribbling away. Then, sanity did an end-run around those defences and was gone. The next sensation was hearing myself, or some stranger, sobbing uncontrollably, and talking through the sobs to that infinite space beyond the trees.

"I don't know how to do this," I told the trees. "I don't know how to be alone. Where the hell are you Tom? I need you *here*."

There was only silence. As I sank back into the chair, I felt a fear that almost loosened my bowels, a fear that I had lost him and I didn't know where to look. I didn't know if he was safe, if he was happy, if he was *somewhere*. If he might even be in trouble and need my help. I had to know. But there was only silence. Not knowing what else to do, I started saying the Gayatri and kept saying it till it was full dark: *Tat savituh varenyam...*

The Gayatri Mantra is an ancient prayer that I learned at the very beginning of our relationship. When Tom and I first knew each other, we spent much of our time together talking, and talking, and talking. He had just returned from two weeks on an ashram in India and had so much to say and to describe. I had been struggling with Eastern philosophy and meditation for a long time and had no one to talk to about it.

Tom told me about the Gayatri. He said it was an ancient prayer recorded in the Upanishads—one of the earliest collections of documents that records humanity's delight in discovering God. Tom felt particularly attached to the prayer; he felt it had a protective power. He asked if I would learn it and chant it with him as part of a meditation practice. I was dubious; my study of Eastern philosophy had been mainly intellectual, detached and had strong Buddhist leanings. This man was asking me to leap into what felt like a foreign country. Also, and it was a very big also, it was chanted in Sanskrit. I have no facility with language and find it difficult getting my tongue around even simple French words. Yet this man expected me to learn an almost unpronounceable series of sentences. But love, stubbornness and great effort allowed me to learn and to chant this magnificent prose poem with Tom.

We said it often: sometimes before meditating, sometimes in times of stress, like the experience of turbulence while flying in a tiny bush plane in the Andes, or while having a tooth drilled. I always found it to be calming and healing and never worried whether it was religious or not; it just was what it was, Tom's prayer. Over the years, we almost forgot about the Gayatri. We didn't meditate as often as we once did. Our conversations only rarely delved into the mysteries of Hinduism or mysticism or meditative techniques. But neither of us ever forgot the words. I would occasionally find myself saying those familiar calming syllables when I was afraid or sleepless. It was a friendly, comforting thing to do. On occasion, Tom would comment that he had had a sleepless night or was trying to sort out a tangled situation and saying the Gayatri seemed to help.

After the stroke and Tom was lying paralyzed on a hospital bed, blind, and with no power of speech, I held his hand, the one that still had some sensation in it, put my other hand on his forehead, leaned into his shoulder and chanted the Gayatri. Over and over and over. I knew he heard. I knew that he was silently saying it with me. The tiny pressure on my fingers told me that.

The next morning an ambulance took him to the Peterborough hospital and a scan that confirmed the worst. There was a bleed in his brain that couldn't be stopped. Tom slipped deeper and deeper into a coma and was not able to communicate anything again.

So that evening, three days after his funeral, after my daughter had returned to Vancouver, I sat outside in the silence, guarded by two watchful Wolfhounds. I started chanting the Gayatri to keep my sanity from deserting me. I kept on saying it, even into the night's darkness.

In the afternoon of the next day I received a phone call from Fay. Fay had been a fellow drummer, had visited Tom in the hospital and drummed for him there. She had been with us at the drumming circle when Tom had the stroke. She had followed me to the hospital and helped me get Tom out of the car. The day after he died she played drumming tapes on her radio show which she dedicated to him. She drummed at his memorial service and later, being a professional storyteller, she told a beautiful and ancient tale.

So when Fay called and invited me to tea, I was happy to accept. We didn't know each other well, but she had a connection to Tom and that made her connected to me.

The next afternoon I walked into her beautiful, light-filled home, just as she was finishing some art work. She said she felt the need for some music that would allow her to stretch out her cramped muscles. She pulled a disc from her massive CD collection. Soon, I heard the lovely sounds of unfamiliar music and a female voice that was compelling and mesmerizing. I lost myself in the rhythm, but in a few minutes I began to recognize some of the words. I listened more carefully; the woman was singing the Gayatri Mantra. The same words that I had been saying for years had been set to music: *"Tat savituh varenyam…"*

I sat down, hard. I felt the comfort and the softness of Fay's presence. After I told her a little about my connection to the Gayatri, she said she had no idea it had been so important to Tom and me.

I struggled with the sense that maybe I was just a crazed, hysterical woman looking for comfort and esoteric meaning in simple coincidence at a time of grievous loss.

But then I let go of all that. I stopped with all the rationalizations. For once, I accepted the simplest and most comforting explanation. Tom was responding to my hurt and to my questions; yes, he was safe, and no, I wasn't alone.

Christmas 2005

It was the first Christmas after Tom died. By early October I was looking toward the "happy" season with a grim anticipation that sometimes bordered on panic. In sane moments I realized, with relief, that at least I would not be spending the holidays at home: I had booked a flight to Vancouver and arranged to have the dogs stay at a friend's.

My daughter and grandson, Jennifer and Gus, lived in Vancouver and they were going through their own Christmas disintegration. Jen's marriage had unravelled after almost fifteen years and they were spending their first Christmas on their own. So we three were going to make a Christmas underpinned by powerful feelings of sorrow and loss but without allowing those feelings to define that time. Without Gus it would have been easy to have a festering Christmas where sadness and pain would fill the days and nights of the holiday. But Gus was ten and he deserved a proper Christmas. Santa would arrive on time, gifts would be carefully chosen and all things "Christmassy" would be celebrated.

During our many phone calls and emails, Jen and I decided that we would get through it not with gritted teeth and tears but with love and spirit. So, lashings of dark chocolate and Australian red wine were called for. My last instruction to my daughter before boarding the plane was, "See to it!"

And she did. For the ten days I was out there, never once did we run out; there was enough chocolate and wine laid on to fortify armies of new widows and divorcées.

Gus had his tenth birthday the day after I arrived. It was a good day: gifts, birthday cake and lots of energetic little boys. We had one chocolate and one glass of wine after Gus finally went to bed. We nodded off in front of the television set as it blared out one last mind-destroying version of "Jingle Bells".

The next day we rushed about shopping for last-minute gifts and the ingredients for Jennifer's famous trifle. She had broken with her mother's and grandmother's tradition of serving a steamed Christmas pudding with caramel sauce after the turkey dinner was demolished. It was a good break; a small bowl of lighter-than-air trifle sat much better after turkey, gravy, stuffing and boozed-up sweet potatoes.

Meanwhile, Gus was trying to pretend that he still believed in Santa Claus and wondered out loud if Santa would remember that he had moved to a new house. Jennifer just raised an eyebrow at her son, and Gus grinned sheepishly and went outside to work off some energy. Jen and I wrapped presents, listened to some lovely music and talked quietly as we did all the familiar things that families everywhere were doing on Christmas Eve. The chocolate and wine supply was dented before we sat down to a light supper.

A few of Jennifer's friends dropped by during that day and evening—women with kids and presents and cheerful affection. No one stayed long, but it was good to see that Jen had great friends who cared for her and who were a large part of her life. My daughter has always had a gift for friendship and I am grateful for that.

Gus finally settled down to sleep by ten o'clock. The rituals had been seen to; the rituals I had done with Jen and her brother, the same ones my parents had done with me: the favourite stories, the hanging of the stockings and the putting out of cookies and milk for Santa.

I must admit that there was an underlying sadness as all of this was attended to. But it was Christmas. Gus was a kid who wondered why his Dad wasn't there and what dying was all about. Jennifer couldn't help but remember other Christmases, other hopes and plans, the fun of playing Santa with a partner. And of course, I was remembering Tom's love of the season, his excitement. I remembered our first Christmas together:

Tom was never able to sleep late on Christmas morning so the first wake-up call was made before there was even a hint of light at the windows. I remembered how, after sleepily sitting up in bed, I was handed a stocking bursting with funny, silly little gifts. We sat there like kids, laughing at our gifts. Tom was delighted with what he found in his sock, but he was much more interested in what I was pulling out and exclaiming over. Just when I thought the stocking was empty, Tom insisted that I put my hand in once again, right into the very toe of the stocking. And there I found a small vial of *Joy* perfume, the real thing, not cologne or toilet water. I think he enjoyed the look on my face as much as anything else that happened that day.

But that was then; this is now. The wine that appeared as the tree lights glowed softly was sipped with appreciation and with talk. There were tears and another glass of wine. I looked at my daughter and there were lines of stress around her eyes and her face held a pallor not natural to her. Her appearance and her voice reflected the exhaustion I felt. When I put my arms around her, and she rested her head for a moment against my cheek there was a reconnection of a circuit that had always been there, since the moment she was born.

But there was another day to get through. *What a way to feel about Christmas,* was my last thought before falling asleep.

Christmas morning was for Gus. Dawn brought an excited wide-eyed little boy investigating new toys, games and books with delight. Santa had indeed been generous. I reflected that a generation ago I would have been on the floor with him, admiring the toys and figuring out the games. But now, those games and toys needed either an advanced degree in mechanical engineering or the mind of a ten-year-old. Gus, also with a child's wisdom, knew that his grandmother's understanding of important stuff—things that could be manipulated on either a small or large screen and usually involved some kind of mayhem, was simply inadequate, worse even than his mother's.

Jennifer and I opened our gifts, drank coffee and ate chocolate. We did well. We honoured the day and the little boy who needed Christmas.

Then we all walked over to church for Christmas mass. The church looked lovely with its masses of poinsettias and greenery. The singing was mostly in tune but the service did little for me. It was a ritual, a necessary one that day; just as all the things we had done in the past twenty-four hours were part of rituals that had gone on for generations. Even the wine and chocolate. They gave us a structure to hang the days on. They kept us grounded in a reality that gave meaning to a devastating time.

The next part of the day did have a modern, twenty-first century twist to the traditional Christmas dinner with turkey and all the trimmings. Dinner that day was at Jennifer's father's home: my ex-husband from whom I had been divorced almost thirty years. He and his wife, Mary, had graciously included me in their invitation for Christmas dinner. Further, Jennifer's newly ex-husband Dan, being closely related to Mary (she was the aunt who had almost raised him as a child) would also be there.

Before we left, I consoled myself that there would be chocolate and wine when we got back that night.

It was a twenty-first century family gathering. Dan, Jennifer's ex, was unrelentingly sullen and uncommunicative. By late afternoon Gus was running on his last bursts of adrenalin and a large dose of family chaos. His world had disintegrated and he had had no say in it. The anger he felt at both his parents began to come out that day.

The day was surreal. At one point during that long afternoon before dinner, Dan was scowling at a football game on television (or maybe it was soccer); Jennifer and Gus had curled up together and were napping; Mary was bustling about in the kitchen, refusing all help, and Pat and I were carefully talking about our grandson, our daughter and the weather. But before we bored each other to death with our careful courtesies, the conversation slipped into a discussion of existential philosophy and the role of religion in the modern world.

Later, we had turkey and stuffing and cranberry sauce; we had sweet potatoes and brussel sprouts and trifle. Everything was beautifully cooked and elegantly presented. Luckily, there was chocolate and wine. I told them stories about Tom; none of them except Jennifer had known him other than a brief meeting at our son's wedding. I was trying to strike a balance between being stupidly maudlin and coldly silent. I doubt that I succeeded but whatever I said, it was received with attention and grace. Bless them for that. I also blessed Mary, my successor once removed, (there had been another wife between Mary and me) many times that day. She is an amazingly beautiful, gracious and friendly woman who was able to make her husband's ex-wife (once removed) feel welcomed. Pat also had the intelligence to marry a woman who could cook.

Finally the day was over. We were back at Jennifer's apartment; Gus had staggered in and immediately fallen into bed. Jen and I turned on the Christmas tree lights and poured some wine. Tomorrow life would go on. If we had all been able to get through today as well as we did, anything was possible. As I put my feet up on the coffee table, Jen said "Another chocolate, Mom?"

As she put some music on the stereo, my mind did one of those peculiar jumps that minds do, and I remembered the tiny bottle of *Joy* in the toe of a sock. It was like getting a hug from a friend who always managed to be around when you needed him.

the weedeater

When I walked into the large garden centre, I knew I had to keep looking straight ahead. I had to stay focused on the task at hand and totally ignore the fact that only a few aisles away there were flowers for sale: flats, cell-packs, baskets, both hanging and flat varieties, and pots of all sizes. I knew that once I gave myself permission to browse among all those glorious blooms of early summer, the fat would be in the fire. I would be backing the car up to the gate and loading it up with all those irresistible plants just waiting to be dug into my overflowing and tangled garden.

But this was to be a no-nonsense trip: I needed a new weedeater and as soon as I found one of those unlovely tools I would be out of there. I found the right aisle quite easily. Just past the garden hoses in all their amazing multiplicity, and then, there they were. Not just a row of implements looking like the one which had just given up the ghost at home: there were electric weedeaters, gas-powered ones of various sizes and power levels and all within a huge price range. I turned from one to another in increasing confusion. It had seemed such a simple task, yet I was feeling not only bewildered and out of my depth, but like a complete incompetent. I didn't even know how to think about making a decision. There were no guidelines.

Almost as though part of me had levitated towards the ceiling, I saw myself reach out and hang on to a shelf. Without it I would have fallen down.

The tears started as I gazed at the row of weedeaters. *How could I decide? This was Tom's job. He knew about these things, I didn't. Why wasn't he here making the choice?*

We might have even had a mild argument. Maybe I would have said, "That one seems very expensive. What's wrong with this one, it looks the same and it's twenty dollars cheaper?"

Tom would have answered, "Yes, but this one is a better buy," and then he would explain why. And part of my mind would be listening, but the other part would be planning where to put the brilliant pink geraniums I had noticed when we first came into the store and whether I needed another large clay pot to put them in.

But none of that was happening today because Tom had died thirteen months ago and my world hadn't caught up. Even after all that time, the pain could sometimes catch me unaware; it would shoot up from my belly into my chest and explode behind my eyes like a jolt of electrical energy run amok. That pain had been a regular occurrence in those first weeks and months but it was rare for it to happen now.

It is as though the body has a life and memory of its own. Just when I think that the cliché about time and healing might have a grain of truth, I would be struck by that sudden piercing pain of loss, of abandonment, of finally understanding that he isn't coming back.

After a few moments, I let go of the shelf, lifted my head and blew my nose. There was a box with a weedeater beside my hand. It looked acceptable; it was in the medium price range and probably had enough power to do whatever might be asked of it. It was also quite a nice shade of green. I carried it to the checkout counter, paid for it and then carried it back to the car.

Later that afternoon, I sat out on the garden swing with a glass of lemonade. Where the pain had been was empty space. Like a room in a house that had been emptied out but a few stray socks had been left on the floor, perhaps exposed when a dresser was moved. I had become used to that empty space. But today, there was a small, determined sense of satisfaction inhabiting that space. In fact, I was almost ready to put the weed eater together; the terrors of flat boxes could be faced with confidence. Afterwards, I knew I would feel the emptiness again, the edges were never very far away, but I was beginning to get a different sense of Tom's companionship, his steadiness, his love.

holding grief

There is no process, no beginning, middle or end to grief.
It just is. And that "is-ness" changes everything.

Living with grief is a mindless sort of experience. Nothing slips into place, nothing is ordered or predictable. No succession of steps to be laid out and pondered over, no grid to place yourself upon. And certainly, no travelogue to watch before embarking on the journey.

Soon it will be three years since Tom took his last trip without me. His journey, if he is still on one, is unknown to me. All I can do is hope that if consciousness survives death, he is safe and finding his home in the sacred. My hope, and often unruly faith, is that consciousness does survive death in an altered but recognizable form, and that Tom's preoccupation with bliss leaves him some time and energy to keep a weather-eye on the ones he left behind; especially the one who is still struggling to accept the whole monstrous business of death and dying and the journey of the soul to regions beyond her ken.

The business of grief and its mindlessness has been a huge preoccupation. Like the experience of claustrophobia, talking sanely or sensibly to oneself in the midst of panic rarely works well. Of course you know that the chances of the elevator plummeting to the basement are almost zero. That is a fact, but one that is totally irrelevant. The sense that the surrounding world is shrinking, closing in, and suffocating becomes intolerable.

Grief is like that. It is a miasma that shape shifts, lightens, almost lifts as time goes by, but is always there, lurking somewhere in the shadows of consciousness.

My grief over losing Tom has finally become an aspect of me. Not quite like the arthritis or asthma that sometimes plagues me, it is not of the same order, but it is not dissimilar either.

There is tentativeness about grief. A choice is involved as to how this frightening, cataclysmic event will be experienced.

Will one deny its power and fill all the corners of life with constant doing? Or will the objective, distanced "one" become the subjective "I" with all its sloppy uncertainties and fragilities? And will that "I" allow this experience of grief to show me other ways of being human? Will I allow a spiritual dimension, one that has been shunted, almost into oblivion, to illuminate a soul I sometimes forgot to acknowledge?

These questions are tiresomely difficult. Sometimes I don't address them at all. I forget. I get lost in the doings of an interesting life. Or I sink into the desolation of my solitary journey. And somewhere between that yin and yang, sometimes in the inertia that overpowers both, I find compassion, or curiosity or humour. And life begins again.

I didn't understand death, couldn't put it in a framework where understanding is possible. The fact of Tom's dying just hung there in consciousness, unattached, unsupported. During the four days of his dying and then later, facing the detritus of death, I wasn't actually there. I was somewhere else, floating, just occasionally bumping against reality. I don't think it was magical thinking, so much as not thinking. Just a closing of the drapes and getting on with things; like cleaning the house before my daughter and best friend arrived from Toronto; knowing only in some darkened corner of consciousness that Tom was dying in the hospital.

It was a disjointed, disassociated time and I have no idea where my perceptive, intelligent and emotional self had gotten to. She was in deep cover.

There are many things about death that confuses consciousness and makes it want to shut down. My mind wanted to know, wanted to believe, that there would be a process. A beginning, a middle, and then an end to the business of grieving. It wanted to believe that there would be a lovely heaven where Tom would be waiting, surrounded by light and maybe a choir. And certainly Wolfhounds. It wanted not to believe in the struggle as life slowly leaches away. It wanted to know, for certain, that I had done everything right. That I had always been kind and forgiving and understanding during all those years of sharing a life. I wanted to believe that when death came we would be so old and decrepit we would just slowly, gracefully fade away. Together.

But there was just a man lying on white hospital sheets breathing each laboured breath until he couldn't. And a woman, his wife, standing beside him, who wasn't really there.

And when I became aware of the woman who wasn't there; when I knew that I was wearing a mask, feeling it pinch my facial bones, how it kept my mouth from speaking and my ears from hearing, and my heart from feeling, I still tried to keep the mask in place with a frantic desperation. I couldn't see or feel, even with blind tentacles, the outline of what was real.

Exploring, then accepting a new reality would have meant reeling in the woman who wasn't there. But there was too much fear to do that.

I Didn't Order It But It Came Anyway...

Three years worth of making a different life.
Finding life, finding death, being surprised, always,
by this business we call grieving.
It involves anger. Also love.
And insanity.
Like leaving a few shirts and his good suit in the back of the closet
for when he comes back.
Three years worth of people's kindnesses. Sometimes misplaced.
Three years worth of doing things just because they needed doing.
Or not doing them. Just because.

Three years worth of loving dogs to distraction. Losing two.
Again to Death.
That implacable sonofabitch who never stops to ask or say please.
Each loss is losing Tom. Losing everyone, everything that ever died.
Three years worth of wondering if I did enough.
Knowing I didn't. No one does.
Three years worth of money worries and wondering
what must be done
and what must wait, maybe forever.
Three years worth of coming home to no one to hold me
and say, you're home.
Three years worth of staying sane, at least most of the time.

Three years worth of growing who I am
and waiting for the flowers to poke out of the ground.
Three years of desolation and sometimes joy.
Three years of nows. Of present moments. Of right nows.
Three years of grief and love.
And sometimes, an amazement that overwhelms me.

compartments

The idea of compartmentalizing is a difficult one for many of us. Something that "Mad Men" and other neurotics with issues tend to do. And the idea of guilt is even more problematic.

One sunny Wednesday morning in October of 2007, I put Oliver, my lovely if vastly overweight Australian Shepherd to sleep. His housemate, Seamus, had said his last good-bye to us only three weeks earlier. My heart was full of grief as I joined a celebration at the Rail's End Gallery after my friend Sarah's first collection of essays had been published.

As a member of her writing circle I was helping to get food, chairs, tables and assorted other things organized. Since I was also part of a women's choir, there was singing to be done. We were there to celebrate this courageous young woman's journey from fear and helplessness after a major stroke toward recovery and wholeness. I felt her pride and her joy. But I also felt the bone-drenching experience of grief.

As the preparation crew gathered, a friend touched my arm. She knew about Oliver and Seamus. She said, "How are you? Really?"

I smiled at her and said, "I'm well. I'm compartmentalizing."

We gave each other a quick hug and then set about the task of filling the empty room with chairs, tables, dishes, coffee urns and finally, platters of wonderful food. We all worked hard, talking non-stop while catching up with each other's busy lives and laughing at the difficulties encountered in that tiny kitchen as seven or eight people tried to organize a party. Steaming plates of food were carried to the other room; cookies were set daintily on china plates, and the half-acre pan of meltingly good brownies was sliced into tiny squares, some of which, the imperfect ones of course, had to be sampled.

The women of the choir gathered for a quick rehearsal and then guests began arriving. Speeches were made, songs were sung, books were signed and the guest of honour glowed throughout. It was a good afternoon.

Later, we cleaned up, put everything away and packed up the food. As I was leaving, another friend touched my arm and said, "How are you?

Again, I smiled and said, "I'm well. Really. But I'm tired and I'm going home to de-compartmentalize."

Those words, compartmentalize, decompartmentalize, had come out almost glibly and with a kind of grim humour. But I think my friends knew exactly what I meant. The grimness as well as the humour came from the fact that women traditionally have said (as one of their major difficulties with the male psyche) that compartmentalizing, the ability to cut off one part of one's life and keep it distinct from another, was a very bad thing. It led to an almost dissociative state where work or social obligations were totally separate from domestic life and tended to become increasingly dominant. The compartment that held family and loved ones would shrink and become more isolated from the other realities.

But there have been changes in how families work and how work has accommodated those changes. As our lives become more complex, we, women and men, are learning that sometimes being integrative involves clarity of boundaries. That there must be separation before integration; a clear labelling of things. *This belongs here and that belongs there.* Then, one deals with bringing them together in a way that is fair both to the *this* and to the *that.*

I am slowly learning about the "this and thats"— how to separate them, how to integrate them. Driving home from the gallery I had a quiet chuckle thinking how "compartmentalize" had become a much less nasty word in my evolving vocabulary. I have learned how important it is to know why and when one is doing it and when to stop. It's the only way to stay whole.

And on that drive home, I also thought about how it was after Tom died. I remembered the memorial service, the lunch afterward in the church basement. I remembered how it was; me smiling with genuine gladness as people came to offer greetings and consolation. I remembered the feelings of warmth, of appreciation and of belonging. The sense that I was embedded in this community of friends and family. Tom was gone. His life with me was over and the aloneness was at bay. Perhaps it was my last great gulp of community before the darkness pulled me into solitude.

So, were those gulps of warmth and companionship a way of separating and building a compartment to hold, in delicate suspension, my carefully wrapped parcel of grief?

Perhaps. Sometimes the mind and the soul will cooperate and become lovingly protective so that the person who aches with loss and grief does not become that loss, that grief. She stays whole.

I had felt guilt after Tom's funeral. That old, *what's wrong with me?* feeling re-appeared, even though so much work had been done and the angst of adolescence left behind. I wondered how it was that I could actually be so sociable at the funeral service. But I knew that I had felt so grateful and overwhelmed as people helped celebrate Tom's life with me, that I reflexively reached back to them with smiles and a deep sense of connection.

At the service, the drumming, the storytelling, the singing from my women's choir and the honour guard of therapy dogs, all celebrated Tom's life. As did his story, the one I had written the day before. As people were leaving, a man I barely knew held my hand and said that it was the best funeral he had ever been to. And I laughed softly, thinking how much Tom would have enjoyed that comment, and agreed with it.

140

But later, the snaking tendrils of guilt started to contaminate a feeling close to joy—a feeling that Tom had been given a loving gift, from me and from his community. I vaguely wondered if feeling joy at my husband's funeral made me a bad wife and a shallow person. Fortunately for me, that worry of not behaving appropriately didn't run very deep. I knew even then, as the bleakness was settling around me, that the capacity to feel joy and thanksgiving in the midst of such loss was an amazing gift. It seems that the human capacity to layer our deepest feelings, to build "compartments" even though they are not watertight, is a hugely important aspect of grieving.

Today is the fourth anniversary of Tom's death. This morning I drummed for him and felt him with me when I took a walk in the woods looking at wildflowers and noticing early signs of blackfly season. The universe, and my own often unquiet soul, felt at peace. Tonight I will go to a meeting of my women's group. I may or may not mention this anniversary because there is much to discuss. There always is. I'm not sure I will want to talk about it. But if I do they will listen and they will care. If I don't, then I will slide my memories into a compartment that allows me to be absorbed once again by quite ordinary happiness.

process: death and my mother's arm

When I was a little girl, I sometimes worried that my mother would die and leave me alone. That particular worry usually surfaced at night after the lights went out and goodnights, hugs and tuckings-in were done.

Then I was alone, upstairs in the darkened bedroom where a small door led to a storage space that we called an attic, but really wasn't. Grown-ups had to crouch to get through the doorway but I always knew it was more than high enough for monsters and other evil beings to get through. They never did, but they could be lurking. I also knew that Mom was just downstairs, knitting, reading a book or listening to the radio, often all at once. And Mom was more than capable of dispatching monsters.

So what to do if she died? The solution my five-year-old brain devised was a plan that seems ghoulish but only because we are considering it with our adult brains. To a five-year-old with very unclear ideas about death and dying it made perfect sense: if Mom died, I would simply cut off her arm and hide it under my bed. Then when they took her away, I would still have a piece of her, to hold on to and to keep for battles with monsters. Even one arm would be enough. I was sure of that.

It consoled me to think that a part of Mom would always be here with me. It allowed me to go to sleep and dream of puppies and games and whatever else five-year-olds dream of. The monsters stayed away.

It is a long time since I've been five. Mom died a few years ago and I didn't think to save her arm. Mom's wasn't the only death; there have been many others. Tom's death left me bereft, without even an arm to console myself with and to protect me from the monsters in the attic. But what I do have is a strong sense of Tom—his personality, so vivid, so strong, haunts me in a way that sometimes leaves me perplexed.

I have extremely unconfident views of the hereafter. The *here* I can comprehend. It is the daily soup that we all live in. But after the *here*? *If I knew what came after the 'here' I wouldn't be 'here' I would be 'there'.* Or so goes my reasoning left-brain. Others have claimed special knowledge, but I, personally, have never known anyone who has been *there* and then come back to *here*. But I will be the first to admit that my left-brain sometimes does get a little out of hand, especially if it is confused.

On the other hand, and there is always at least one other hand if not three or four; I have that persistent sense of Tom, not in the abstract, but in the here and now. A sense that he is still available, still here (or maybe there) with a comforting presence that just misses being tangible. When I reach out my hand it is as though I just missed him, that a moment ago he was where my hand is now. He feels only a breath away, only a heartbeat from *here*.

One night recently there was a severe storm. The trees bent double under the terrible lashing of the wind. Then the power went out.

I found candles and the "snake" flashlight I wear around my neck. I knew the storm was coming so the dogs had water, the kettle was filled and there were a couple of pails full of water in appropriate places. There was a collection of candles, lanterns and flashlights on the kitchen table. Electronics were disconnected and windows were closed.

I knew I was safe; I'd done the right things, but I felt a few tendrils of panic around my core. My mind felt sound and sensible but a little wired, a little frayed around the edges. At times like that, solitude is hard. The connections are gone.

It isn't that Tom was particularly great at minor disasters. Not at first anyway. He would never remember to organize water and find a couple of workable flashlights before a storm struck. But eventually he would have the oil lamps lit and have the cute little speakers attached to the Walkman radio so we could hear music and news. Then he would start rooting in the workshop for the Coleman stove in case we needed it for making tea. Eventually, even if the power was still out, I would fall asleep knowing that all was well. Tonight, I have no idea where the Coleman stove is or what to do with it even if I did find it.

But I can live without the Coleman stove and the radio with the tiny speakers. And I know that I can deal with sick dogs, storms and problematic septic systems. There may be much that I cannot do around here, but on the other hand, there was much that Tom couldn't do either, especially during his last two years on earth. Between the two of us, we worked out plans and we managed.

For a long time the loss of my co-planner and my co-manager was overwhelming. Sometimes it still is. But, to cope with that sense of being overwhelmed, I have discovered a perennial secret that is so simple that it is almost embarrassing to mention. Maybe I'm even the last person in the universe to discover it, but here it is. Love works. Love folds me into Tom's spirit. It speaks wordlessly in the quiet times, the times when I listen for the brush marks he makes on my soul, the brush marks that keep me connected to life as well as to death.

Grief is not sustainable as a single definable state. Like every human experience, it is not static, nor immutable. If I were to hold on to grief, define my existence by its massive power, then I would need to do it deliberately, consciously choosing dark over light, death over life. Tom would be appalled.

Grief is a tsunami. It is powerful, destructive and overwhelming. But then it moves on. It has changed the landscape in its path but it does move on. The sting of loss still happens and can catch me with an unexpected spasm of pain. But there is also, often at the same time, the undeniable presence of love that connects me to Tom.

This presence isn't one of awe, the beat of angels' wings or the sound of muffled organ music. If there is music, it will be the "Hallelujah Chorus" (the music that erupted from the speakers the moment Tom and I said our wedding vows), or more likely, something by Willie Nelson or Bruce Springsteen, Tom's traveling music.

There is warmth and a cradling; a peaceable stillness that heals the hurt and allows hope a foothold.

A large part of missing Tom has been rediscovery of him, but also, perhaps, of God. It is difficult for me to feel a strong connection to that word and what it represents, even when I consider Her feminine aspect. It's like trying to get a handle on infinity, or the Milky Way, or a quark. But Tom has been a gateway to a sense that there is a something or a somewhere outside the bounds of ordinary consciousness where I feel his presence or his love. He was there, sitting beside me on the hard wooden seats in the open railway car that brought me up into the mountains of British Columbia last year. He sometimes sits beside me on the garden swing and I feel enveloped by his peaceful presence. Or I might be throwing clothes into the washing machine, watching a turtle climb out of the pond onto the large slab of granite that slopes into it. Or I might feel a simple wash of pleasure from being alive in the world. Or its opposite. And I will sense him nearby, just out of reach, but not far away. I feel his humour, his generosity and his compassion. Sometimes I can even imagine God as a much larger, much grander version of Tom; as his background or under-painting.

Maybe that's enough. Maybe a more sophisticated idea of God will have to wait until later. In spite of missing Tom, I am not in a great rush to leave this difficult universe, so I rather hope that my full enlightenment comes much later.

spiritual trekking

This story would not be complete without speaking of that long struggle between the dizzying suspensions of both belief and disbelief. The questions and the tedious second guessing became consuming as I wandered between watery faith and an uneasy lack of same. But the occasional sense of finding a home in the transcendent kept all the doors open.

Religion, the more focused and muscular arm of spirituality, is at its best when it sheds light on ways of exploring and sharing our fascination with the mystery of existence. Often we find its unique beauty in poetry, art and metaphor. But often our own shadow and its contrariness, becomes a need to destroy or diminish or to become lost.

So this section begins with a fable where the shadow, that often disconnected, negative but vital part of ourselves, the part which complicates all our earnest striving towards the light, is personified.

Sometimes the shadow needs to come out of "Shadowland" and perhaps, take a bus trip.

The Bus

Once in a while my negativity needs to go out for an airing. It creeps and slithers its way out of Shadowland and into the bright light of day. Soon it finds its voice, and a large serving of self-importance. It learns to doubt, to disparage, sometimes even to say mean things. It gives voice to anger and frustration. Even desolation. It is especially good at giving fear a voice. The fear that often lurks in my subconscious despite being larded over with hope and happiness—those unlikely and suspicious emotions from the Light Side.

She has a personality and I call her Negativia. She is a dark, craven creature wrapped in darkness. She, and for now let's give her a feminine face, can misbehave, misspeak, and be a great burden to the someone who lives on the right-hand side of the Enlightenment Bus serenely waiting for the world to evolve, waiting for bliss. She who needs to wake up. Unlike the dark one, she doesn't know that bliss is not a permanent home. Not yet. There is too much work to be done.

The story is an ancient legend (although I may have made it up this minute). The dark one, Negativia, is a great aggravation to all those who hop onto the Enlightenment Bus looking for a pleasant, relatively uneventful journey to the Land of Enlightenment. Because she also has a ticket to that very same land on that very same bus.

The legend, those wispy bits that still survive, also concerns a smiling, robust young woman who calls herself Sublimia. She boarded the bus at the stop called, "Here You Are Weren't You?" full of expectations and a wondrous faith that she was finally on the right bus and going in the right direction. It was an old red dinosaur of a bus belching out oil and noxious fumes. But the destination sign in the front window was correct: "Enlightenment: Hop On, Hop Off".

She took a seat by a window trying to avoid the fissures in the cracked leather that hurt her tender bottom. She made herself as comfortable as possible and gazed out the window, peacefully watching and waiting for the world to evolve, waiting for bliss. Sublimia was happy and content. She had had a long, tiring journey with much more to come, so it is understandable that she nods off. But, she picked the worst possible time to sleep.

Because, as she slept, a stranger boarded the bus. A stranger who had been waiting at a stop called "East Gotcha". It was Negativia and she was wrapped in darkness. Unnoticed, she took a seat a few rows behind Sublimia. Reaching under her cloak, she pulled out a small briefcase. Opening the well-worn clasps, she took out a simple blow gun and lifted a cover to expose a secret compartment where her portfolio of remedies was stored. She noticed that the vial labelled "Anger" was almost empty (a trip to the hidden aisles of Costco was in order). She dipped a tiny dart into a vial labelled "Fear". She fit it carefully into the blow gun. She fixed her attention on the sleeping woman sitting a few rows ahead. She took aim and fired. And waited.

A few moments later the robust young woman called Sublimia signalled the bus to stop. She slowly stepped out the back door when it opened for her. Fat tears rolled down her face as she silently watched the bus disappear around a bend of the road. She was too frightened to continue her journey. She looked back in the other direction, the one she came from, but there was nothing there to return to. On either side of the road the forest was deep and dark and frightening, probably full of lions and tigers, snakes and spiders. But the woods would give her protection, hide her perhaps from the nameless dread she felt in the depths of her soul. A place to stop for a while. To wait. And that is where the story has its first ending. Sublimia standing by the roadside, irresolute, wondering if she had made a huge mistake getting off the bus. Wondering what had happened. Not noticing the dark shape that had got off the bus just behind her.

Like many legends, this one leaves us wondering if S and N will meet again. If S will find Enlightenment, if she will discover that N has a few very useful darts in her portfolio. If they can accommodate each other without the fear and dislike that is usual for them.

I know that my own dark side, that slithery shadow, is obnoxiously out of control only when I ignore her, pretending she isn't always there, hovering in the background with her little briefcase full of darts. Because if I don't recognize her and acknowledge her strengths, her gifts to me are anger, fear, jealousy and despair.

But I do have a few remedies at hand to recognize and integrate that shadow. For me, the shadow often emerges as a bone-deep lethargy, a disinterest in everything that was of great importance just yesterday. Other times, it is a deep unreasoning anger. Or a fear that my best will never be good enough. But sometimes the grace of compassion flames into being and I will find it impossible to be lethargic, angry, or judgmental.

And sometimes, along with it, there is laughter. Humour can shift the frame, allow lightness or a cocked eyebrow to demolish the self-importance of rant and righteousness—especially my own. It can slow down the descent into apathy or anger, or fear by opening up an off-ramp.

Faith is another remarkable antidote. Not necessarily faith in a benevolent God because atheists can have faith, but a belief that pushes absolutism aside, allowing for the humanity of productive doubt and the possibility of some new thing. Faith allows for a shift in consciousness, a shift that can say, "But on the other hand."

Images of travelling, of struggle, of light and darkness and the toxic darts of fear, anger and distrust are important metaphors for me. They help me learn how to be human. I have spoken of Negativia and Sublimia, dark and light. Their playful or vicious dialectic can affect my notions of who I am and where I am going. But sometimes, thankfully, they are quiet.

the enlightenment bus

Winds have been high for two days now. The trees are no longer fully dressed. The golds and browns and rusts and burgundies now carpet the forest floor, soft and earth-smelling.

I woke up this morning to see a brilliant orange ball cresting a distant hill and for a moment my breath stopped. It has been five months since I have actually watched the sun rise—not since the trees and underbrush suddenly transformed themselves into a living forest of green. A beautiful welcome after six months of minimalism and winter white. So I had forgotten how, when the branches are bare, the early sun can fill my small house with golden light and warm me by the time I have breakfast made.

It is very mild for November and Luther the dog, Gypsy the cat and I have been enjoying this unexpected gift. They, Luther and Gypsy, have been searching fruitlessly for frogs at the edge of the pond. But frogs have long since burrowed into the mud where they will stay in damp hibernation until spring calls them back to life. The turtles who dotted the sloping granite rock face that borders the western edge of the pond on warm sunny days have also disappeared into hibernation. The leaves that speckled the surface yesterday have sunk, becoming a giant argyle blanket covering the pond's murky bottom. The glassy surface reflects dark tree trunks, clotted branches and the deep blue sky of fall. The only movement is the slowly drifting clouds with fluffy white edges and dark centres.

Emerging from this peaceful meditation on nature, I become aware that I too am part of this landscape. The part that has become self-conscious. Nature played a wild card when humans emerged from the swamp. We became conscious of things like the difference between good and evil, of death as well as life, and the conundrums of choice and freedom. All those philosophical and theological issues that our brand of consciousness can dream up.

For example, we often like to say: "Well, on the one hand, but… on the other hand." Maybe the difficulty is simply that we are born with two hands. *Would the problem of dualism be less problematical if we were "uni-handed"? Would I be less likely to argue with myself?*

Probably not, because the separation, analysis, and identification of things helps us to understand an important dimension of the world—such as remembering things, doing math, making outlines and plots for stories, and for some of us, grasping the principles of thermodynamics and relativity. But understanding the *meaning* of these things requires me to let go, temporarily, of dualistic thinking and accept that there is a unifying principle that connects the frogs in the pond to the stars in the sky and to me. And I can surrender to that intuition which I grasp in those lovely moments when stillness overflows and spills from my self-awareness outward into the universe.

But then, slowly, like a ghostly shape rising from the mist in a bad movie, the other hand emerges. Beckoning. Pointing to a boldly printed sign saying: "This Way to the Real World."

And then I'm off. Into the doing and the counting and the judging, the evaluating and the separating, one from the other. Yet, those things too are a part of being human. So when I hear (or read) someone saying to me, pedantically, petulantly or passionately, "You've got to get out of your head." I feel the pressure of a button being pushed—the one that says: *React now!* I am working on disengaging that button but with limited success. Should I curl up behind a kidney? Perhaps get lost in the intestinal coils when I get "out of my head"?

I think I know what is meant by "getting out of my head". It means to stop thinking, judging and questioning, to be more open, more accepting, more intuitive. And that sounds bloody marvellous. Who wouldn't want to feel more loving, more blissful and more oceanic? But I'm still back with the head; maybe even the "bad" head that needs to think and judge and evaluate and question. And then, someone, something, perhaps the other hand, will say, in a sensible tone of voice: *Of course you don't get rid of the bad head. You just need to teach it to know about limitations. The head has a tendency to become arrogant and imperialistic. It wants to become the "Grand Poobah" in charge of everything. Heads like dogs and children need to learn about boundaries.*

I agree. Of course. The love I feel for the earth, the compassion I am sometimes able to feel for its people, are deeply rooted somewhere near my heart. The head's job here is minuscule. In fact, the head will probably nod wisely if asked and say: *It's not my job man; let the heart look after that stuff. My job, says the head, is to jump up and down when I think it necessary, and to say "No". For example, that person over there, the one who seems so wise and enlightened, he wants you to go down a path that is littered with other people's heads and hearts. That "wise and enlightened" being wants you to reject all that doesn't fit his criteria for enlightenment— that much maligned term.*

But how, in the name of that enlightenment, can I become *one* by severing that part of myself that allows for a quality called discernment. The very quality that permits the integrity of the soul. The quality that always balances the needs and gifts of the mind with a compassionate and surrendering heart.

I cannot "get out of my head". My two hands, or all those paired opposites like body and mind, yin and yang, left brain, right brain, need the balancing discernment of my soul. The transcendent factor that helps me to know that dualistic thinking is a valuable tool, not a way of being in the world. So, the trick is, if I can call this spiritual balancing act a trick, to stay centred, mindful and aware of all my realities, so that I don't feel that I have fallen off the "Enlightenment Bus". Because when that happens, and it does fairly regularly, it means that I have

152

fallen off that exquisite balancing point where everything is contained in the moment, where there is no afterward or before. Where there is no striving or reaching for the next rung on a ladder that is just out of reach. Forgetting that there is no rung and there is no ladder. Spiritual ladder climbing belongs on someone else's bus.

Almost every religious or spiritual tradition teaches that a "still point" may be reached through the development of a spiritual practice involving quieting the mind. I am working on that. Much of the work involves self-forgiveness, since despite my intention to spend early mornings in a meditative state, I often find myself sloping off into my usual morning routines which may or may not involve a few minutes of quiet communion. But feeding the animals, building the fire, washing the dishes, give shape and definition to spiritual life. They are its bones. But it has taken me a very long time to understand that.

notes on a journey

The idea that I am on the downward side of a ferris wheel ride, knowing that so many others have exited, one-by-one, sometimes two-by-two, tipping forward and walking away from the ride, is an absurd but oddly comforting image.

Death does not seem to be playing a large part of this aging woman's dance with sadness. It is rather the slowing down, the betrayal of the body and that existential dread that everyone used to talk about: the dread that nothing matters very much, that there is no over-arching theory or purpose to life, no god to whom we must be accountable, no meaning that isn't absurd and no reason that we should even exist.

Those are some of the ideas I wrestled with many years ago when I first began my fascination with philosophy; that branch of learning where earnest and cerebral people try to understand what it all means. Some scholars make a lifetime pursuit of this work while others need to let it go and wash the dishes or have a baby or write a poem. Or, to crash open the door leading to an existential leap of faith that leads to a notion of God. Lately, like an addict staring at a bottle of wine sitting on a kitchen counter and wondering whether to take that first drink, I find myself meandering, spiralling back to some of those questions I thought I had left behind so many years ago. So, in spite of the doing and the feeling and the sensing and the leaping, I always come back to the thinking. Perhaps it's a curse.

From time to time, bits and pieces of ideas or philosophies or "thinkings" get written down. Sometimes I think they seem to be a loose framework for how to live my life. Sometimes I think that I just need a real job. But the reading and the thinking and the writing are a large part of the package that is me; the package that has been me since I left the Catholic church and discovered do-it-yourself thinking. That world of ideas can be a frustrating one; it can be deeply humiliating, but also exciting, joyful and satisfying. It has led me from Ayn Rand (the ex-Catholic's first saint) through existentialism, phenomenology, Zen Buddhism and many other "isms" and "ologies". And the writers who fill my bookcases: Camus, Sartre and de Beauvoir, Carl Jung, Ram Das, Pema Chodron, Thich Nhat Hanh, Kathleen Norris, and Thomas Merton. And of course, all the breaks in the thinking, the counterbalance to it, was the journey of meditation: discovery of the "not me" and the exploration of mind and not-mind.

Many of those thinkers magnetized me. The philosophy that first pulled me into looking at the underpinnings of life's basic questions, after a very brief flirtation with Ayn Rand's objectivism, (remember "Atlas Shrugged?") was existentialism. This was the philosophy that arose in Europe between the wars and I discovered it initially not through the abstract and ultra-rational works of Sartre and Husserl, but through the wonderfully lyrical and emotional essays and novels of Albert Camus. Then came the heavy-handed rationalism of Jean-Paul Sartre. "Existence comes before essence" was his clarion call and he wrote over a thousand pages explaining what that means, how being arises from nothingness, how that fact gives us a terrible freedom: terrible because we must create who we are every day of our lives.

There is no template, no eternal soul and no God. So whatever we do or don't do, whatever we become or don't become, is dependent on our own will, our own conscious independent choices. And if we don't make those choices as fully conscious beings, then we act in bad faith, we "forget" who we are and sink into a life lived without integrity, without freedom. We are what we have become and no super conscious "being", no creator of souls or essence has anything to do with it. There

155

is no meaning except what we create; no essence except what we distill from our own lived experience.

Phenomenology, a way of looking at the world and at existence that preceded and led into existentialism, advises us to stay with "what is", stay with "the thing itself" as its proponents Husserl and Heidegger were fond of saying. Otherwise, one is led astray into "isms" and false beliefs of all kinds—the worst one being mysticism. Staying with "the thing itself" focuses the mind on what is being considered. It demands a strict detachment from opinion, prejudice and any pre-conceived idea of our own or the surrounding culture.

And when I, an eager philosophy student, discovered these two disciplines, I was entranced. Finally, a way of understanding the world, a way of finding meaning that didn't depend on anything except what could be seen and explored by my own mind. No priests, rabbis, ministers or even teachers were strictly necessary. Nothing need be accepted on faith. No reliance on doctrine, either of the church or society. Each individual person, in beautiful autonomy and silence, could be Columbus exploring what it means to be human.

As I deepened my studies, my understanding, and often my confusion, I discovered Zen Buddhism. Its methods were undoubtedly phenomenological and once again, I was entranced. Zen Buddhism wasn't a religion; it didn't postulate God every time a conundrum appeared. It taught a way of seeing and accepting the "is-ness" of things by meditating and getting beyond the limits of rational thinking. Getting beyond thought, how amazing that would be. I was suspicious at first. I had been trained to think that there was nothing beyond thought except for a swampy, limitless bog where no sane or intelligent person would want to go. But, I bought a ticket anyway and set off on a trip into the "limitless bog".

One of the first stops on that branch of the journey was my discovery of the Sufi stories. And the story that will always stay with me was the one about the rug seller who priced even his most beautiful and precious rugs at no more than one hundred coins. A curious buyer asked him why he didn't charge more. The rug seller said, "But there is no number higher than one hundred!"

Well. That story triggered my own search for a number higher than one hundred. It cracked open, just a little, the door leading to a possibility that would lead to a different kind of knowing, to the existence of synchronicity, to the possibility of consciousness beyond the boundaries of my own mind. If that consciousness exists, then there might be space for metaphysics and an epistemology different from what Father Flanagan taught of those matters in Theology 101. And a world view that would be very different from the atheism I had lapped up from Bertrand Russell. Finally, there would be room for weeping, for love and for laughter. For a while, in my earnest rummaging through all the philosophies and belief systems that I could tackle, I had forgotten how important those things are.

Discovering that the absurd could be funny, that doing the dishes or raising a child or making love were as important as the search for enlightenment, allowed me to stop searching for meaning in books and philosophies; it made me realize that knowledge, understanding and meaning could come to me in a moment of serendipitous grace, in a fit of indigestion or while working in a garden.

This journey doesn't have an end. I'm not "there" yet and I don't know if there is a "there" to get to. But the new philosophers, the new theologians, some at least, are digging deep into the fertile soil of the new paradigm; the one where you can count past one hundred. Where God laughs and weeps. Where we are not ignorant sinners waiting to be saved. Where we look at teachings of the many spiritual paths that point beyond dualism to oneness. Where we see the "other" as part of ourselves. Where we see the shadow, our rejected or dark or unconscious selves, as holding a key to the mystery of being. And finally, where love and compassion become the water in which we swim.

further notes

Many years ago my primitive, childish self was imprinted with a dour theology that said I was a weak and sinful creature and only through the tortured death of a magnanimous God who became man could I be saved from the fires of hell. This God (man) was nailed to a wooden cross to die in agony because I was evil and must be saved.

Eventually, within my lifetime, that doctrine was not so much dismissed or even watered down but pushed to the back burner of the theological stove. Many churches got rid of the bloody, suffering Christ figure and went with a bare cross. Then guitars, in the more modern congregations, replaced organs. The fires of hell were dampened down and then extinguished. Original sin was pushed to the back of the closet along with indulgences, novenas, and the Thirty Days Prayer. The theology didn't actually change very much but the emperor's new clothes seemed to disguise a lot. My church became someone else's but it didn't matter because I was long gone.

I think I might be embarking on another sea change. But I feel like an obnoxious little kid lying on the floor, kicking her heels and screaming in a very loud voice, *I don't want to go! You can't make me!* But something has me by the ankles and won't let go. I'm getting tired of kicking and my voice is hoarse.

Sometimes I speak to God. Sometimes, She answers. Sometimes I speak to Tom and sometimes he answers. Sometimes I think I am delusional.

Being just one step away (and I hesitate to say either up or down) from atheism or its less shrill cousin, agnosticism, this is a paradoxical situation. Often I just don't know what to make of it except that sometimes, when the oddness happens, there is a soft sense of love and comfort and kindness in the world. That is all I need to know with any certainty.

I am beginning, just barely beginning, to build, despite all evidence to the contrary, on a fragile sense that the universe is underpainted with an indelible wash of compassion and bungee cords of relentless connection.

Sometimes my rationalistic, judgmental, in-the-world self totally objects; how banal, how simplistic it says. It would call me a foolish virgin except that the noun is inappropriate. But what "Miss nose-in-the-air Rationality" doesn't know, or forgets, is the old saying that says: "They who persist in their foolishness will become wise." So I persist.

Slowly, glimpses of the sacred appeared in my peripheral vision. There were times, usually when I was surrounded by trees and rocks and water, when there was an odd sense that I can only think of as presence; a presence that felt like a gentle gathering , a pulling together of the life all around me—growing, greening, gnawing, flying, singing, climbing, scurrying, slithering, eating, defecating and reproducing. Life being life. And it would feel not only purposeful but all of a piece, the wholeness of being, just that, just there. And I am there in the midst of it all, inside and outside, both, at the same time.

All of that, that awareness of unity, of life extravagant and overflowing, surely must be the foundation of theology. Or religion. Or philosophy. Because that extravagance of being also includes the instinctive compassion that reaches outward, beyond the judging, the evaluating, the greed, the self-absorption and the cruelty. Beyond even all notions of what could be and what couldn't be. Beyond it all, is the sense of the sacred. The beginning. Again.

the God quest

Writing of the complexity involved in Irish atheism, Nuala O'Faolain said, "Nostalgia and wistful hope are far, far more powerful over the human heart than the dry pleasure of having a perfectly logical position."

Perhaps it is just and inevitable that I became a reluctant believer. For all the years that I called myself atheist, it was always with some difficulty. I was a "regretful" atheist. Perhaps it was my Irish heritage that held me back from fully embracing it. I knew that there was something more than flesh and bone, callipers, scales and other instruments for measuring and weighing and naming. Even the existentialists, whose books I devoured, found meaning in the midst of the meaningless void. They celebrated the instinct to create without measuring or defining it.

There was much for this regretful and rather doubtful atheist to investigate, to wonder about and to rub the sore spots that were my legacy from Catholicism. And there were many sore spots.

Just as a fish is born into water and never knows the medium that hosts its relentless swimming, so I was born into the Catholic Church. It was total immersion, total acceptance and total obedience. Rules were explicit: no petting below the waist with your boyfriend, and no eating meat on Friday. For Catholic girls these rules were much more important than the more abstruse doctrines like the mysteries of the Holy Trinity and transubstantiation. It was all absorbed, the easy and the difficult, with our daily bread and the Sunday Eucharist. There was nothing to think about. Just as a fish swims, a Catholic girl prepares herself, as her most important mission in life, to follow the commandments, love God, obey the priest, her parents and her future husband and raise children for the glory of God and the church. Is it any wonder that so many of us disappeared into a blind, rebellious rage?

My reaction when I recognized the arrogant rigidity of that hierarchy brought me to a place where I became incapable of seeing beyond my anger. The gentler, compassionate side of the religious reality disappeared from my perception of how the world works. It is a long time since I have been a Catholic girl. I could no more return to Catholicism than I could to girlhood. And yet…

The winter of my fifteenth year, I went skiing every Sunday at Camp Fortune, a ski club just north of Ottawa. That meant attending the 7:00 a.m. mass at Ste Anne's, the old, musty, French Catholic church just up the street from where I lived. The dark was deep and wintry as I left the house and I heard my boots crunch over sidewalks packed hard with snow.

Once past the heavy wooden door of the church, I became enveloped in the transformative world of Catholic worship. Teenage angst and its consuming worries were left by that great door. By the time a hand was dipped into the holy water font, every sense was soothed. Only a handful of people would be scattered among the front pews: myself in ski pants and boots with a parka thrown over my red ski sweater, and darkly contrasting, a handful of old ladies in long black coats, heads almost hidden in colourful kerchiefs. Also present, were the priest and a sleepy-looking altar boy.

Since this was pre-Vatican 11, the priest had his back to us as he leaned over the altar murmuring the words of the mass in Latin. The richly brocaded chasuble, red or mauve or green, would be glowing in the candlelight. The enormous chandeliers hanging from the ceiling were mostly unlit but the candles supplied a soft, luminous radiance that satisfied my adolescent yearnings for peace and beauty. The corners of the church remained shadowy; the ghostly, larger than life-sized statues were silent and watchful.

Only the quiet Latin chanting of the ancient words of the Mass broke the silence. All of us, the old babushka wearing ladies and my brash adolescent self, were brought back to the ancient mysteries. The faint smell of incense, the wax from the candles, and the polish used so lovingly by the women who cleaned the church, became the scent of holiness. Rhythmic chanting became its sound.

In time the priest turned to us and said, *Ita Missa Est* (Go, the mass is ended.) We left our pews, genuflected, and went outside to a wintry morning that was showing the grey light of dawn. The mass was over and time began again.

Sometimes I pray. In spite of myself, in spite of the logical and tough-minded person who lives is me. In spite of not being sure to whom the prayer is addressed. Sometimes I am thrown back to the beginning. To take another look, to start another great trek backwards. The loneliness of the long distance pilgrim is a burden, especially when the starting gate keeps reappearing on the horizon.

What keeps me at this, like a particularly stubborn dog with a bone, is not a sentimentalized view of childhood experience. Sentiment doesn't take you very far from the moment and is unhelpful during the hard parts of the journey.

Is it my own soul or "higher self" (or better half perhaps)? Is it an entity often called God who represents all that is unknown, mysterious and just other? Is it an imaginary entity, like your younger self's imaginary best friend who was always there, always in a good mood, and always let you have the biggest half of whatever was going around?

Today, reading Thomas Merton's poetry, I am overwhelmed by his love and joy. And something in me leaps up in response, leaps with an answering love and joy. Whatever it is that leaps, that is what I call my soul. And I would like to nurture it so that response will happen again. But after that simple analysis of soul work and what I might cautiously call the transcendent, I am lost again.

I could saddle up my untrustworthy old nag called "Logic" but I know that he will suddenly come down with a cold, or so he will say. But he lies. He knows that the terrain I ask him to travel has too many impossible chasms, caverns and downright scary bits for a cranky old horse to even consider travelling.

So here I am holding this radical Cartesian doubt in one hand but knowing that there is another response in me that is true and undeniable. And that response points in a direction beyond logic, beyond the everyday, beyond even simple happiness, comfort and love. It includes all of that but goes beyond. So what is this "beyond"?

One doesn't pray to something called "the beyond". In the movie *Shirley Valentine*, Shirley, one of moviedom's most appealing characters, would talk to her kitchen wall whenever she reached a crisis point in her life. An odd thing to do, but maybe that was her "beyond". My kitchen wall is just a kitchen wall but, on the other hand, I haven't tried talking to it yet. It seems that the transcendent could be in any or all parts of the mundane.

Music, poetry, the sudden bursting greenness of a tree, can trigger a joy that bumps me to a place beyond ordinary human perception. And with the joy comes that living, breathing sense of loving connectedness with all that is, or was, or could be. The mystics, through the centuries have referred to it as the oceanic sense. The psychologist Carl Jung called it the transcendent experience. St. Teresa of Avila just said, "Do whatever brings you most to love."

When joy, love, and that felt sense of the sacred come together it may be my beginner's attempt to understand God. But, in five minutes I will be doing something ordinary like paying bills, feeding the dog, washing the dishes, and I will forget that I know all this. The trick is to pay the bills, feed the dog, wash the dishes and remember that there is, or could be, love and sacredness even in the dishwater and the dog's dish. (Luther the Labradoodle often reminds me that there is particular sacredness in the dog's dish.)

This often stony heart, the one that closes itself around a kernel of doubt like a greedy fist around a coin, will admit how it is an oyster trying to cope with an irritating grain of sand. And for me that grain of sand is the legacy of Catholicism. This particular legacy (gift or curse) provides easy access to pervasive guilt and a lingering addiction to absolutism. It may also endow one with an ear for sloppy theology, like that of a musician who can detect a flat or off-note from a hundred paces. For example, I have finally realized why so many of the books and the language of current and best selling gurus of pop spirituality are offensive. It is not the retreaded ideas or the paucity of language; it is the triteness, the pious jollying and the careless intermingling of sacred text and symbols to create a spiritual smorgasbord limited to white bread.

religion, spirituality and bicycles

The words "religion" and "spirituality" are so packed with meanings and associations that my psyche automatically primes itself for a possible allergic reaction. "Religion" seems a more straightforward, soldierly kind of word. If someone says that their religion is Catholicism or Hinduism or Judaism, then I have a reasonably clear idea of what they mean.

But I have a niggling distrust of "spirituality" with its New Age connotations. It tends to leave a syrupy taste in my mouth, there is no bite or substance to it. The word often seems to refer to a Disney-like smorgasbord of watered-down beliefs. These belief systems that evolved over centuries of disciplined thought and practice from many philosophical and religious traditions are not so easily understood.

Every genuine spiritual tradition has explored and developed a framework for the "dark nights of the soul". The times when doubt and aridity take up residence in the soul. The times when concepts of pure white light, heavenly bliss, God's love or the redeeming power of prayer are lost in the bleakness of despair or grievous loss. The flounces of New Ageism have little to say of these vital matters.

To speak then of spirituality or religion is to open a hornet's nest; I am conscious of the need to walk very softly and not to carry a big stick. I can only speak of my own religious and spiritual experience (while trying not to use quotation marks) and hope that they resonate with something that is universal. I often walk in a spiritual fog, but as long as I keep my wits about me and don't hurry too much, I find a way to where I need to go.

For me, religion has always been a conundrum. It is so hard to unpack that word and look at it with an unjaundiced eye and a non-skittish brain. When Tom was in the hospital there was never much hope that anything could stop the haemorrhaging deep in his brain. So he just kept slipping further and further away from us. I screamed my grief, my horror and my anger at a placid sky. I begged whatever spirit was alive in our world, whatever beings were tuned in to Haliburton, *to let him live. Don't let him leave me alone.* Yes, I was selfish in my grief.

What I didn't do was go to church. I didn't turn to the religion I had been raised in. Religion had nothing to say to me. Even if it did, I wasn't listening. Whatever meagre solace I found was in the spirit of the people around me, in their faith and loving kindness, as well as in the rituals I learned from Tom. Like saying the Gayatri Mantra a hundred million times until my teeth chattered and my brain went numb. But I never looked to religion.

But maybe religion is a bicycle. A bicycle that carries our sense of the sacred, of the holy. Maybe out there in the universe are billions of bicycles waiting for riders to find them and pedal off.

Because bicycles are everywhere—leaning against barns and outhouses, at the bottom of ditches, in the undergrowth of forests, half-covered in the sand of the earth's deserts, propped by a sink of dirty dishes, just outside a room where a woman is being raped and beaten. Sometimes they are even in the shadowy regions of churches. They are found at the gateways to the world's most appalling ghettos, in the back wards of hospitals and in their operating theatres.

Perhaps I mislaid an important truth during those awful days at the hospital and beyond: that there is always a bicycle parked nearby. It is always in good repair, sturdy and ready to travel through the universe and out through the door of space and time.

When Tom died, I felt that somehow my skin had been removed. I was so naked and so cold. But a day came when I felt pedals under my feet, that I was moving. I just didn't realize that I was on a bicycle.

The God quest can be simply a way of organizing spiritual yearnings, a transportation system for our longing to reach the mystical, to name the unnameable and to find a way through the creative forces of chaos. Out of those places of confusion, of numinous love, or blind fury, we may need a useful method of giving form to the formless.

But as we pedal away towards eternity, destination enlightenment, the wisest and most mystical of teachers know that we must always be grounded in the basic stuff of our world and its demands. Otherwise we might be moved to follow the maunderings of the mystically demented or the treacly "feel-goodisms" of New Age leaders who have found shortcuts so as to avoid the dark.

That darkness is as important to the life of the spirit as food and water are to the body. Those days and nights when we sink into the pain of grief or loss or abandonment are times when the soul can hear its own voice. These periods of grief need not always be pathologized into clinical depression or mental disequilibrium to be medicated away. They may be times of incubation, of stillness and fragility and are part of our ongoing and creative humanity.

Religion, at its best, honours the mysteries of the dark, of the dimly seen. The expression "dark nights of the soul" came from the Spanish mystic, St. John of the Cross. He wrote beautiful commentaries on the transformative powers of darkness. A more modern writer, Thomas More, has written on the ability of failure, depression and soul-deep doubt to open our hearts to a deeper vision that will lead us back out into a world that is fundamentally changed because our perception of it has changed.

I am still struggling with finding the way out of the labyrinth of that dark night; still trying to find the thread. Just when I think it is wrapped tightly around my hand, it slips away and I stare, again, into the relentless dark. The night is still there.

For me, accepting the dark involves holding the tension between two opposites until I feel that I am breaking in two. Those opposites might involve career or relationship decisions, or the more tenuous arena of soul work. But eventually, sometimes slowly, sometimes in an instant, a "third thing", neither choice A or choice B, appears out of the chaos, fits itself snugly around my soul until I know, without a whiff of a doubt, that this is right. This is who I am. This is what I am meant to do and to be. And it is so blindingly simple that I wonder why it took so long.

Then I am called back to the mundane by a problematical septic system or by the teeth-clenching antics of an ill-favoured off-spring. But for a moment or a day or even a week, the glory of being in just the right place at just the right moment, the joy of being a whole human being, overshadows everything else.

And the cycle begins again. I become trapped in the complexities of the ordinary, of the mundane. Usually I hide for a while (often in the pages of a novel, mysteries are good). If I am feeling more energetic, I indulge in a rare bout of housecleaning where everything must be scoured to some point beyond mere cleanliness. That burst of energy usually is short-lived. Then my mind becomes restless again. It must pick up an idea, something abstract and indefinable like the nature of the universe or of God is good, and worry it.

Thinking about the nature of God can be like picking up a piece of knitting. There is nothing more mundane than the homely art of knitting and nothing more soothing for hands that need to do something. Sometimes it just seems to be the right and the necessary thing to do. I usually have something in a cloth bag parked somewhere in the living room. It contains an endless scarf that may never be finished, patterns for complicated items (like socks) that are way beyond my skill level and will never be made or even attempted, and bits and pieces of work that were started and then abandoned. But the endless scarf is always there.

I picked it up last night while I listened to a summer storm rattle the windows and sluice enough water off the roof to float an ark. The lightning illuminated the work as it flowed through my fingers and it felt a little like saying the rosary in a darkened candle-lit church, when I used to do such things in such places. Feeling the beads of the rosary slip through my fingers, and feeling the soft wool yarn transform itself in my hands into a woolly scarf seems innately satisfying.

I work on the nature of God in the same way. She may be in the yarn, the scarf or my fingers but I strongly suspect that Her traces are in the doing and in the being—the knitting, the knitted and the knitter. Sometimes, when it all comes together, the needles click rhythmically and my mind wanders into the soft places of loving kindness where there is grace.

Like knitting, my thinking about the nature of God is working without a pattern so that I never know just where I am or where I might be going. But now, finally, I am not concerned. Most of the time I can balance my need to know, to be able to say something sensible about the nature of God with the wonderfully calming knowledge that it doesn't really matter very much how much I know or say.

Because you can never know it all, never assemble all the arguments, all the big and little miracles of everyday life and make them come together into a cohesive theology that answers all the questions. Even the ones I don't know enough to ask. To do that would take me out of the universe we all live in and into another unknowable realm where bicycles and knitting are unnecessary.

Most of the time I am comfortable with this uneasy assumption of ignorance. I love this world and am not yet ready to leave it. Not even for Tom. I pick up my knitting for consolation, not just to complete another scarf. As far as God is concerned, I think about Her in the same way. Knowing that there are no final answers in my cosmology, no definitive bit of intelligence that will close the circle, no absolute epistemological truth to be uncovered, I rest in my unknowing and I am content. I can't knit socks and I can't know God. *Amen.*

Like Kris Kristofferson (and many other musically inclined people) I believe that whatever gets you through the night has much to recommend it. But I also need to look for integrity in the methods I use to explore big questions like: *What must we do about the fact of our existence?* So in meandering through the field of current spiritual writing I listen to my inner ear. I listen so that I can hear the false notes, the too-easy answers, and the language that becomes maudlin. But I also listen for the words that ring true when one soul tries to speak of the sacred from her own reality from her own pain and her own joy. Chances are there will be no numbered steps leading to bliss, no magical mantras or prayers, and no borrowed rituals to be used as window dressing.

Catholicism may be wrong-headed, bloody-minded and arrogant. But as for its theology, it is *rigorously* wrong-headed, bloody-minded and arrogant. It has standards; sometimes it even has an awful elegance. And it knows how to touch the soul through the senses. Quite a legacy. Combine all that with original sin, fragrant beeswax candles, incense and Schubert's "Ave Maria" and a child is marked for life.

Recovering Catholics (and others marked by ritual and a profound theology) need to find a way that brings us to the sacred, provides solace during life's agonies, and rest for the chattering mind. I have experienced anger, even hatred at times for the church. I have been incensed, appalled and sick at heart by the posturing and obscene behaviour of the clergy and their hierarchy. But I miss the rigor of ancient theology and the grace of Catholic inclusion.

By inclusion I mean the community of people, intent, if only sporadically, on greeting a being, energy, or force, which represents the best that is in them. That community also includes the dead, people who were loved and have a place in our hearts and lives. In prayer we acknowledge them and hold them close. And when one becomes rapt in prayer or contemplation, a sense emerges that we are part of a sacred trust, part of God. And when I look at God I am looking at the heart of meaning, the heart of all that needs to be understood, the heart of all that could be but isn't yet. The heart of human possibility.

final (for now) God thoughts

There is such stillness today. The air is drenched with moisture and covers the land with a heavy transparent blanket. The leaves on the trees are limp, a bird is trilling and once in a while, a late hibernating frog remembers its vocal cords before tunnelling into the mud at the bottom of the pond. These are the only sounds. And they are muffled. My mind knows that I am far inland but I expect to hear the depth-sounding sonar from a distant ship. It seems a good day to think about God. The stillness seems to echo in my inner landscape. It is hard to resist the quiet.

Yesterday and the day before that and probably the day before that, I have been reading about God. It is quite astounding the number of ways that have been discovered to talk about God. It appears that this is a subject that has titillated, frustrated and obsessed humanity since time and the regarding of time began. There are those who would say that the study of God is the most important task in life. Perhaps so.

But I still keep shuffling the God cards.

Perhaps I need to stop the shuffling and wrap myself in a sense of the sacred however and wherever I find it. Luther the dog is quite sure it resides in the bottom of his food dish or the cookie jar holding his treats. Or in a good satisfying belly rub. Maybe we two-footed ones need to stop trying so hard. One of the ancient Zen sayings tells us that enlightenment is an accident and all spiritual practice can do is make us more accident prone. Perhaps knitting and bicycles can help.

Many of us develop a spiritual practice before we decide on the existence of a deity. Or a "Transcendent Reality". The belief that God is in me and I am in God can be helpful. It indicates that we have a spiritual dimension that is as real as a body part. I can't imagine someone proclaiming that they don't have a left leg as they go stomping about the universe with both legs fully operational. But I digress. Theology is not as simple as that. Legs are material. I can reach down and feel them, even whack them till it hurts if I am still uncertain.

The God decision is a primitive choice. All the thinking, the discussions, and poetic head-banging appear to have little impact on this choice. If the decision reverses itself, as it occasionally does, there may be a drawn-out process of research, of consultation, perhaps hand-wringing is involved. But there comes a moment, just before total exhaustion sets in, when there is a sense of being lifted up, whipped around and instantly, reality is changed. I might in fact hear a joyful voice lustily proclaiming, with soul shaking certainty, *YES, I AM*.

But an alternate experience is possible. Then the voice I hear is saying: *Dammit, just give up on all this mystical silliness. There is no Transcendent Reality. It is all just a dream of wishful thinkers and frightened little men and women.* And I can go back to sleep.

I am still shuffling the God cards.

In spite of mind-numbing doubts, the cards often re-arrange themselves into a kind of crazy tapestry of ancient Catholic rituals with Buddhist principles and practices of being and of living well. Most days that seems to work well. I embrace the wonderful expansive now and accept the "is-ness" of things as they are, right now.

But sometimes I think about death and what happens next, about an alleged God of compassion, about faith and grace and Hail Marys and the Gayatri Mantra. Historically, I have dipped, sometimes double-dipped, into a variety of spiritual feasts. Tasting, with great relish here, rejecting there, always moving before fullness (or indigestion) could set in. In my favour, in recent years I have moved between only two feasts, two tables. First, the ancient, mystical and honourable faith of

Christianity, the wisdom of the Desert Fathers, those early Christian hermit monks who went into the desert to wrestle with their souls and with their God, expresses that tradition beautifully. As does the memory of a little girl, stopping on her way home from St. Brigid's School, ducking into a silent, noon-time church, and sitting in a front pew to keep God company for a few minutes.

The other feast is the one offering the compassionate simplicity of Buddhism. Buddhists don't bother themselves with the idea of God, of heaven, or whether there really is a white light leading the newly dead to a reunion with pre-deceased loved ones. It is all irrelevant because Buddhist belief centres on how to live within the principles of loving kindness, of compassion for all beings. Of how to live up to your edge and then push it, just a bit, gently.

The rituals of many other faiths, their ceremonies, are graceful and colourful and full of meaning, but they don't speak to me in a language that my soul understands. They don't pluck at my emotions or at whatever region of my soul is responsible for creating and holding meaning. I have puzzled over these things for a long time. Why the beautiful and evocative rituals of native peoples or Hinduism or Islam or Judaism may move me but are unable to reach that meaning-making place in me. And it isn't for lack of trying to understand, accept and incorporate them into my spiritual life.

The answer for me may lie, at least partly, in historicity. For a ritual to truly touch that place of meaning and stay there, it must resonate with all the many times that event, those words, or that act has become not just a part of the past but a part of who I am. The Catholic Church is no longer in my life but it has given me a legacy: the smell of church incense, the sound of Eucharist and Angelus bells, Gregorian chant, beeswax candles, the ancient Latin hymns, the thin papery feel of the pages of a prayer book in my hand, the taste of a communion wafer in my mouth, the splintered, glorious light coming through stained glass window, the sense of communion with all those sharing a pew. And most of all, a feeling of wordless awe and gratitude, a sense of how everything is all of a piece, all one: one pulse, one breath, one essence.

And now, the stillness of the pond envelops me again. I am a part of this landscape, this spiritual and physical place where I am, where the silence is. The Catholic church pointed a shaky finger at the silence and then, to paraphrase a Buddhist expression, it mistook the finger for God. The long trek backwards is, I suspect, a journey home to pack a small suitcase of things I can't leave behind.

Part Six
Disruptions, Epiphanies and Peace…
(repeat)

leaving home

I am getting ready to leave this house where I have lived for ten years with Tom, assorted dogs and a couple of cats. And all of this readying brings me closer to saying goodbye; a goodbye I have been dreading but also anticipating with a measure of relief.

Several friends, well two anyway, advised me to make sure that my ambivalent feelings were not blocking the next move. So, this week I have been sitting quietly in various places in the house and on the land, gathering my own energy and the energy of all the lives who once lived here with me, and still surround me with their presence: memories of joy, of laughter and of awfulness. The trees in the forest that surround the house on three and a half sides are, as always, benignly present. The huge maple tree shading part of the deck and my bedroom is now showing some of the glorious colour that will become glowing and luminous in the coming weeks. The great pines and the spruce with its standing stones standing squarely in the middle of the back yard are archetypal in their pull.

If I shut my eyes I can remember, exactly remember, the pounding, rhythmic drumming, as Irish Wolfhounds flew around the property. Their flight path started on the deck just outside the door, then they would take a flying leap up the steps, under the cedar and ivy covered arbour, a right turn around the vegetable garden another right past the workshop, right towards the big maple tree, back to the deck, and then around again. After a few laps, tongues would be hanging out, eyes sparkling, and it would be time for belly flops on the deck with legs splayed and contentment radiating from their ungainly selves. In later years there was less running and more napping in the sunshine, but always, those great shaggy heads and smiling eyes were never far from me, companionable, affectionate and amazingly funny. I miss their joyous, graceful presence but I feel their spirits and their energy, too powerful to simply disappear forever.

And of course, more than anything, there is Tom's spirit in every inch of this place. I look at the large stones that surround the little pond beside the deck. And I remember how angry I got when I saw him heaving those boulders into place. He of course paid no attention; he liked demanding physical work and was not happy with nagging wifely interventions.

I can also see Tom doing obedience training with Seamus on that long stretch of grass between the vegetable garden and the back fence. The two of them were a team, affection and trust in both their faces as they moved through the paces required for the obedience ring. Sits, stays and long downs were effortless after a few weeks of training, unlike my attempts at dog training when my only successes happened when the dogs took pity on me and decided to do whatever it was I wanted them to do—just to humour me and because they were kind, good-natured beasts. If I had enough dog cookies, they would do their best to impress me with their smartness.

I remember how Tom would carry up the many bags of manure and pails of compost for the gardens. He would pound in poles for the tomato plants so they would not keel over when they became heavy with the weight of the vines and the fruit in August.

As I was turning a corner this morning, my eyes were caught by Tom's tacky shelf. This shelf was in a relatively hidden area of the house and it held all the silly, touristy souvenirs he dragged home from our holidays. There is a glass paperweight with a toothy piranha inside, a tiny green plastic bus overflowing with people from Colombia, the miniature steel Eiffel Tower from France, the little white Parthenon from Greece, the blow gun from Venezuela and the hairy Highland cow (steer?) from Scotland. Even though I laughed at these things when he brought them home, they will come with me wherever and whenever I go.

A lot of baggage will be left behind, given away, sold or brought to the dump when I leave. But the memories, the spirits and even the damn silly statue of the Indian dancing girl and the papier-mâché Mexican guitar player will come with me.

I know that not only is a place being left behind, but the part of me who lived there, that vital fragment of who I am, has been set adrift. Her tether is still back with the Wolfhounds and Tom and the big old maple tree.

Yet, I have done this before…

The first time I left home I was nineteen and confident that the world was about to become the best it could possibly be. I was a brand new bride. The wedding had taken place in the familiar church where my parents had been married and St. Brigid was the saint in charge. The reception was in the garden surrounded by leafy maples and summer phlox. I wore a size seven confection, simple and elegant. My new husband, age twenty, looked slim, handsome in his white tuxedo, and vaguely apprehensive. He was wiser than me. I was too caught up in the last line of every fairy tale, the one that says how they lived happily ever after.

The reality that I was actually leaving home and beginning life as a grown-up person didn't sink in right away. There was no honeymoon because my new husband was in the midst of a course that would turn him into a meteorologist, and my first teaching job was waiting for me in northern Toronto. So we postponed a honeymoon that never actually happened.

That first night, our wedding night, in our new apartment, after perfunctory (and painful) lovemaking, we were both, God help us, virgins, the groom fell asleep and I sat up most of the night staring out the uncurtained living room window at a strange mid-city landscape wondering what on earth I had done. Fear latched on to my heart and lungs and stomach and soul. What had I signed up for? What was this new life that I had eagerly hurled myself into with all the stupidity, stubbornness and enthusiasm of your average nineteen-year-old?

Now, more than forty years later, I can still remember and feel that fear twisting my gut. These days, most days anyway, I am eager to begin the next chapter, the next adventure. But sometimes, usually around 4:00 a.m., little toothpicks emerge whose job it is to prop my eyes wide open. At those times fear and worry blot out the lust for new chapters and new adventures. But I know the anatomy of fear as well as its genesis. I know that leaving home, finding a new place and solving problems—like where I shall put my bottom when I need to find that peaceful sense of being home, will be a challenge, not a roadblock.

There were many moves, many home leavings before I realized how important it was to find a place in a new home where that sense of comfort or ease could be found. That place always involved a comfortable chair, a notebook and a pen. There must be room for a coffee mug and a place for books to pile up. There must be a window with a view, a sense of nurturing solitude, and a place to put my feet. It is what a soul needs so it can unfurl itself and sink into stillness, into solitude, and yet not feel alone.

But this time, with the next move looming, the apprehension feels different. Maybe because this is the first move that I have made alone? Maybe because there are so many other uncertainties in my life? Maybe because part of me wants to stay here with the ghosts and the memories? Maybe I'm afraid of being alone in a strange place? Maybe I'm tired of starting over? Maybe magic has exited the world?

Looking at all of that, and allowing myself a third cup of coffee as I absorb it, I feel the subterranean rumbles of something I can only identify as an entity called "faith". (I have met this creature before and it may not be trustworthy.) It seems to be rousing itself from its stupor.

"What the hell is going on?" says this cantankerous old beast. "I don't know how you keep losing me when I'm so large and so embedded that you can't take a breath without me. Whoever said 'Oh ye of little faith' must have had you in mind. I am so much a part of who you are that I can't believe that you forget me. But you do. So this is what you must do."

"Imagine a chair, say like the one you're sitting in right now, the one with the lovely orange silk cushion. Imagine the little brown hassock your feet are on; the blue mug you have just put down; the blue notebook and yellow pen. Look to your right, out the window you sit beside; see the wall of trees with their brilliant red and yellow leaves and blue sky beyond. Imprint this picture on your mind. Now, is it impossible that these defining features of your "place" won't re-form themselves somewhere else? And wherever that new place is, will there not be a comfortable chair, a vista with trees and sky, a blue notebook and a good pen?"

And then there was silence.

So I am here, gazing out the window, glad that faith, that terribly ill-defined quality without which life is not possible, has spoken to me. Like a sleepwalker about to career over the brink of despond, that profoundly rooted but often forgotten entity called faith has given me a pinch of reality. I will remember this place. I will remember other places. And then, at the right time, a special spot will announce itself, one that will allow everything to come together again and a new old place will create itself. And then I'll be home.

Somewhere, in this unknown new place, there will be a comfortable chair near a window with a view of trees. A notebook, a mug of something, and a good book will be close by. There will be a dog large enough to trip over and with eyes capable of love lying close to the chair. Life will once again wrap itself around me and the music will begin again.

God's agent

July 10, 2008

There are layers upon layers of Catholicism that even now, decades after going into recovery, I am still uncovering.

When I was growing up, Mother had a small pantheon of saints who all had specific roles and tasks assigned to them. St Anthony was the finder of lost objects; St. Jude was in charge of resolving impossible or lost causes (my mother consulted him a lot about her daughter); St. Agnes, always had a lamb tucked underneath her arm in her pictures (she always reminded me a bit of Anne Boleyn and her head) and she had a particular passion for music and music lovers; St. Christopher, recently demoted, was always taken along on journeys as protector from all thing dangerous such as running out of egg salad sandwiches on the way to anywhere; and St. Ann was the friend of restless virgins who desired a different state of affairs. In fact, I now remember the bit of doggerel she inspired: *Good St. Ann/Send me a man/Good if you can/But please, send me a man.*

Since I was raised in a strong Irish Canadian culture, the "good" probably referred to someone who "wasn't to the drink taken", who could hold a steady job and who was not likely to indulge in indictable offences. I vaguely remember St. Joseph as the saint who took a particular interest in maintaining happy, holy, Catholic families, a sort of Catholic household god.

But in the last thirty or forty years I haven't given much thought to these busy saints as they go about their appointed tasks. That is, until last Saturday. In the midst of a keynote address at a writer's breakfast, the speaker, Dorothea Helms, told the story of how her sister, in deep distress at not being able to sell her house, called her Aunt Mary, the family's repository of wisdom, esoteric and practical. Aunt Mary asked only one question: "Have you buried St. Joseph yet?"

The sister, after recovering from the shock, replied, "No, wasn't it done all those centuries ago when he died?"

Aunt Mary, not one to tolerate smartass answers, told her in a severe tone what she had to do. "Go and buy a statue of St. Joseph and bury him in your garden. Your house will sell."

Since Aunt Mary's wisdom was never to be doubted, the sister did as she was told. The next day, a family came to look at the house, liked it and bought it.

I chuckled to myself at this story and later with Dorothea as we exchanged stories of growing up Catholic, although neither of us had heard of St. Joseph's real estate talents. But since her sister's experience, she has heard many similar stories. I told my friend Judy about these bizarre happenings. Even though she was raised a staunch Presbyterian, she said, "Oh yes, I've often heard of that, and people say it works."

I was fascinated by all this and a little dumbfounded. Since I am in the process of selling my house in a market that seems to have flat-lined, I was open to any idea that might help to sell my wallflower of a house, a house that no one had asked to dance even though she looked just as pretty as a picture. So shutting up the little voice that said this was all superstitious nonsense, and deciding that no stone should be left unturned, I brooded on the next step: where to find a statue of St. Joseph in this small hamlet of Haliburton, a place not known for religious idolatry. So I turned to the internet. Within seconds I discovered "St. Joseph.com". And there was a link to St. Joseph and real estate. There, in plain view, was St. Joseph, the purveyor of "St. Joseph's House Selling Kits" for only $9.98.

Of course I ordered one; how could I not? The site promised delivery in ten days or less.

I have started to pack.

October 24, 2008

Three and a half months ago St. Joseph, Tom and several deceased dogs were given an assignment, two assignments in fact: to sell my house and, in due course, to find me another.

And then, nothing. Appropriate advertising was done, nice pictures appeared on the internet, and many people actually wandered through.

"What a nice house!" they said. "So much privacy, we love the property. Lovely landscaping. And the furniture is beautiful."

But no offers were forthcoming. Maybe people were just being polite. The price was lowered, but the market had become flat. I was in the middle of a calm as still as the Sargasso Sea. Then, in early September, like a slight breeze, there was a flutter in the market. It was strong enough to bring more showings of the house and many people came through the house. But then, another lull.

This time I took action. Rather than just polishing the taps and fluffing the pillows, I lit a candle in the early mornings, when the house was still, and focused on how it would be to leave this place. I said goodbye to all the corners of the house, to the land and to the ghosts of all the beings who had dwelt there. I told Tom and St. Joseph, if he was still listening, that it was time to go. What he needed to do was to find us just the right place (a list was appended) and then to get us there. All the dog spirits, the ones who had lived and played and loved us in this place, were to help. Because, after all, Luther the brown Labradoodle was their successor and he was a very good dog.

I practiced this odd business of talking and praying and focusing through September and early October even though there were times when I felt more than a little foolish. But on October 6, an offer was made and accepted, a good offer, not great, but adequate. On Friday the seventeenth, the offer became firm. The house was theirs.

A few days later, I submitted an offer on a small stackwall house full of windows and light, sitting on seven-and-a-half acres of maple, beech and hemlock trees. It faced south towards a large spring-fed pond where great slabs of granite sloped into the water. The house had no appliances; the kitchen and bathroom had obviously been designed by a guy who didn't care about aesthetics or even convenience; but I couldn't stop thinking about it.

I took a deep breath and put in my offer, hoping that the builder/owner would not be insulted. Just minutes before the offer expired he signed it back. Still too high, but within my personal stratosphere this time. I signed it back again; he accepted. I had the house and the land. And the pond. Or at least the bank and I would have them soon. I also had a huge dose of anxiety.

The house will be almost maintenance free and is energy efficient with its sixteen-inch-thick mortar and cedar walls. It looks as though it just grew where it is. Inside, light pours through but there is room for only a minimal amount of furniture. There are no closets. Challenges lie ahead. Sigh.

But I think I shall live there for the rest of my life. Luther and I have tramped the trails, in awe of the maples and the hemlocks and the pines, but mostly of the stillness.

A mantra has just announced itself to me: bring little, remember gratitude, and forget the rest.

Faith

I've come to this place
a thousand million miles
from where I was before.

I've come to this place
where
the gravity of
trees
shelter
watchful birds.

Granite rocks slice
into shining water,
debris tucked
neatly
into murky bottom.

I've come to this place
where faith is
a dog, a cat, a book,
a fragrant fire.

I've come to this place.
I've come home.
A talisman against the loss
of elsewhere.

coming home

May, 2009

Sitting here in my usual place by the window, a book lies open in my lap; occasionally, I read a few sentences. A blue spiral notebook is on the table beside me; occasionally, I write a few sentences. Otherwise, I gaze at a pond cradled by the hemlock and hardwood forest. The granite outcrop slopes downwards on the pond's western edge and the sun picks out the rose markings on its ragged top edge. A pair of songbirds trill seductively, and in the shadowy bays and inlets of the pond, young tadpoles ponder transformational theology.

On my side of the window the dog Luther lies stretched out on the floor like a hairy brown rug needing to be vacuumed. Gypsy, the other four-footed member of my household, is practising her stalking skills on Luther's tail, twitching as he drifts into the stage of rapid-eye-movement sleep. It is a blue and gold and green morning and I am inhaling peace.

I am starting a third season in this new home in the forest. The snow and ice of a long bitter winter slowly became spring which then slid into summer. Unpacking, arranging, re-arranging, and purging has taken place. Carpentry has transformed this beautifully minimalist cabin into a home where I can stow my clothes and winter boots and put the blue dishes on open shelves in the kitchen. New towel racks holding yellow and white towels and a medicine cabinet are attached to a wall transformed by yellow paint. New flooring covers the cement, although there was some regret since the bright terra-cotta paint caught the colour of the cedar in the walls and made a wonderful background for the turquoise blue and burgundy rug Tom and I had hauled home from Turkey. The computer and its accessories have taken over a quiet nook between the kitchen and living room.

But it is in the cedar-lined, light-filled sunroom, the room that stretches across the front of the house, where I live most of the time. One end of this room is where I sleep, with a wide day bed which was beautifully constructed by friends with large talents and big hearts. Deep windows flank two sides of this wonderful bed. A small bookcase built by my father to hold my Bobbsey twins books sits at its foot and my grandmother's beautifully carved walnut table with one wonky leg serves as a bedside table. Close by is another old table with candlestick legs, an untidy pile of books on it and a deep comfortable chair. A mug of something is always nearby and there is an orange cushion. This is where I read and write (grocery lists and poetry) and gaze out over the pond and into the forest.

The room is bisected by the front door which is flanked by wooden hooks for jackets and coats, messy but utilitarian, as is the pine wood box on the other side of the door. Beyond all that is my dining room with an old scarred table that still glows with a patina of golden light. The deep blue and yellow wooden chairs around it were painted a lifetime ago when I was immersed in a short lived but manic spirit of folk art. It lasted only long enough to complete the orange and brown and yellow birds that perched on wobbly paint strokes on the seats of the chairs. The chairs are scarred and a little beaten up looking (there are teeth marks on their legs from long-ago puppies) and I often have to re-glue those legs, but they still hold people's bottoms, even wide ones, with comfort and a crazy kind of style. When I sit there, at the same table where I have sat at for twenty years, I am looking out, past the pond into the forest.

Even in deepest winter the sun warms this room as soon as it gets itself above the horizon and sends long fingers of light and warmth through and then over the hardwoods. By the time I move with my coffee mug in hand over to the deep chair with its footstool, the sun has warmed that end of the room. And if the sun is not available that day, if the sky is grey and the clouds dark and fat with snow, then there are lamps and the heat from a woodstove burning in the living room to keep me warm.

But I am idealizing, just a bit.

Yes, this little house in the forest truly feels like home but there are days of difficulties and even despair. Ice, snow and freezing rain storms were happening almost every day when I first moved here. The newly installed washing machine had caused a tiny but annoying leak the source of which could not be found. So for a week I mopped floors, five times a day. The firewood which was promised to be seasoned for two years, wasn't. So there was much smouldering and sulking in the woodstove. Boxes were still piled all around, and finally, what had begun as a chest cold, turned into pneumonia. And it was Christmas time. And I was alone. Not an auspicious or even mildly happy way to begin a new life.

But after spending Christmas afternoon in Haliburton hospital, physical and emotional recovery began. Friends, new and old, turned up with soup, hammers and energy. They put up shelves, moved boxes and unpacked them. Enough soup arrived to float a small boat with enough left over to fill my freezer. Good Samaritans hauled a load of dry wood up the driveway in large sacks because it was too icy to get a car close to the house. The plumber finally found the leak and dryness was welcomed into the kitchen. A large wood bin was built just inside the front door by the same friends who had created the bed, and that meant I could have a two-week supply of wood drying at a time.

My gratitude to my friends, some of whom I barely knew, was boundless. Their decency and compassion and willingness to do what was necessary remind me that the world is not without hope.

Many dark nights (and days) were to come when I wondered at my passion for being here, when I doubted my ability to cope and when I felt old, abandoned and sick. Those were days when I looked out my window and saw only more snow, more whiteness stretching into infinity and where the trees looked stark and foreboding.

There was no sudden and wondrous transformational moment where everything changed, when light and hope and beauty became my lens for viewing the world. But instead, a gradual settling in happened; a settling of the house around me and me into the house. I learned to trust not only in the efficacy of friends but in my own. There still were, and are, days of stress and even bleakness, but never a time when I didn't know that this is where I need to be. That first winter passed into a spring filled with remarkable wild flowers, leeks, warm days and blackflies. Summer arrived and I discovered the joy of stillness while sitting by the pond with the frogs and the resident animals.

Faith is an unruly creature holding both light and darkness; sometimes it is slippery and unreliable, sometimes demanding a leap into the unknown with no guarantee of a safe or comfortable landing. But my reliance on faith has brought me here. In fact, has brought me to most of the places of my heart, both the hard and the healing places. I can't describe the dimensions of this creature; I can only know its footprints.

November, 2009

The blazing colours of autumn are past, and looking out over the pond, I can see deep into the forest. Colours are muted and the stillness is unmarked by birdsong or the papery sound of leaves moving high on the branches of maple trees. A thin, wrinkled skin of ice formed on the pond early this morning. It was melted by noon but soon the ice will thicken and snow will erase its lovely contours.

I am getting ready for the long northern winter with a little anxiety, but trusting that the firewood is dry and will burn well over the next five months. My car has good winter tires and I have spiky things to slip over the soles of my boots on icy days. There is plenty of food in my cupboards and, always, a bottle or two of a decent wine tucked away.

Just in case. In case there is a storm that knocks out power and makes roads dangerous for a few days.

There is a certain satisfaction in getting ready for winter. There is also satisfaction in having plane tickets to take me to Vancouver for Christmas, where the weather may be wet and sullen, but mild.

This is home. I don't always know with certainty that all will be well. In fact, I know from sorry experience with houses and all they contain, that it is rare when all is perfectly well. But if it isn't, then I'll think of something. Or my friends will. And that is enough.

faith

The winters up here in Haliburton County, a summer paradise for cottagers and resort guests, are long and usually hard. This winter, though less cold and snowy than usual, we had a four-foot dump of snow over three days in early December. It took a week to dig out. In January, a thaw came, with two days of rain and the large pile of snow on the flat part of my roof, shifted downward. So for many weeks I had a rather lovely curl of snow that slowly slid down over the edge of the roof and then, with a sudden overnight deep freeze, stopped. The curl of snow had turned into solid ice and had descended far enough to block almost half of the front windows.

Fearing for the safety of people and animals walking to my front door, since the occasional large chunk would break off on a mild day, I went at it with determination and a strong metal shovel but not much skill or strength. Sometimes frustration leads one to do stupid things. My so-called good shoulder joint and rotator cuff was a painful mess for many weeks. So the shoulder injury combined with the usual aches, pains and frustrations of winter, called into question whether the beauty and deep peace of the landscape, the joy of settling down with a book on a snowy afternoon while watching and feeling the warmth of a leaping fire could compensate for the difficulties of living here. I began to doubt my ability to sustain a life here.

So I started thinking about apartments, maybe a co-op in the city. Maybe an apartment here in Haliburton would become available. Maybe it wouldn't be so bad; it would certainly be easier. Probably more sensible. So, disconsolately, I began looking in the Toronto papers and thinking about contacts and all the wonderful things about city life that I used to love. Concerts, plays, funky restaurants serving food still unknown in Haliburton, coffee shops, cheese shops, and Yonge Street. But my enthusiasm stayed tepid. Toronto, any city, isn't home any more. And the idea of an apartment, even up here, seemed depressing.

But one morning, not very long ago, I woke up with a soul full of hope. Nothing external had changed. My shoulder still hurt and my back was telling me I had done too much lifting the day before. But a shift had happened. Another feeling/sense/thought was brushing itself into consciousness. Perhaps a dream had pursued me through sleep. Something had shifted at the edge of awareness; another roomier dimension had opened up. That sense of doom and weakness was disempowered. I wasn't going anywhere.

I meditated that morning with a very specific purpose in mind. I calmly laid it out for Tom, just in case he hadn't been paying attention, and for any other benevolent spirits hovering nearby. *Tom, you helped me find this place, you helped me get here, now, help me find the courage to stay here.*

I knew that there was work to be done; the body as well as the soul has to become as efficient as it can. I have slowly begun to make changes in how I eat and how I exercise. I am seeing a good physiotherapist and actually doing what she tells me to.

One morning last week as I was eating breakfast, I heard on CBC radio that mortgage rates were going up. I called the bank and made an appointment with their mortgage person. I quickly got dressed, put Luther in the car (he is a calming presence) and drove to town. An hour later, I took a deep breath and locked in my mortgage for seven years. I'm here to stay.

Sunday morning going up

Sunday morning. I am here in the sunroom that faces south and has large windows on three sides. I am looking out over the frozen pond and the trees, seeing what I have always seen since early December: snow, mounds of it, acres of it, so many shades of white, sometimes glistening as though someone threw diamond chips, truckloads of diamond chips, all over the surface of the world outside my window.

But today the snow is melting and looks lifeless. The temperature has been above zero for three glorious days even though many of them were rainy or overcast. For the first time, I can actually see the outline of the pond with its still frozen but now watery surface visible: it is individuating itself. Everything is waiting. I hear the crows calling their raucous promise and, even though there are no visible signs, I know, with a giant leap of faith that life is just waiting to emerge.

So this morning I told Luther the dog that someday soon it will be spring. He looked interested but bored; first, because English is his second language but second, because he has forgotten that up here in Haliburton County we actually don't have a "uni-season". Eventually winter does end. So I told him that one day we would look out the window and see no snow and no ice. The pond would have water. *That is snow that melts Luther. Imagine a huge drinking bowl with frogs and plants and a surface that ripples in the wind and, if you drank without stopping, you could never come to the end of it. And when we get tired of watching the pond, we could walk through the woods looking for wild leeks...*

I have no idea what a wild leek looks like but it sounds like a wonderful thing to do in the spring. *And on our walk we will see the palest of pale green enveloping the maple and beech trees, the most glorious, softest colour in nature. There will be branches lying on the ground blown down by the many wind and ice storms we endured over the winter. You will carry one around in your mouth Luther, teasing me until I grab it and throw it as far as I can. You will rush off, ears and tail pointing towards ecstasy, to find it and then tease me again.*

We will push dead leaves out of our way looking for tiny new sprouts of plant life, and I will wonder what they are. The baby fern fronds that curl in such lovely symmetry won't be up yet, that will be for a later walk, but we will see other newly alive green things. I have just found a field guide to local plants so I will be sure to carry that around so we can identify some of those growing green things. Or not.

And we will probably see and hear birds; this is their busy season. Singing, mating, house-hunting. And they will sing their songs of joy and longing as we gaze up through the branches of the maples towards a sky so blue that it will hurt our eyes.

I make a mental note to find a field guide to local birds. In my ignorance, I only know birds by colour and size and song. They don't have names and that has never been important to me before. But now it seems that naming is something I need to do. Luther, of course, feels differently but he may already know their names.

We will probably find a fallen log to sit on, at least I will. Luther will continue to explore. He will probably find a wet boggy spot on the forest floor. He will come back with muddy paws and a silly grin.

And then we will come home. We won't need a fire to be comfortable; the sun will warm us as we lie on the daybed— Luther dreaming of slimy frogs, me listening to a cello concert and half reading a book.

Soon Luther. Soon.

Those wild leeks are happily growing their tiny muscles; the silent frogs are coming out of REM sleep where fat flies buzz eternally; the slowly warming earth is breathing in all that snowy wetness so that once again there will be spring.

Soon Luther. Soon.

life at walden three

April 14, 2009

There's nothing like being awakened at 6:00 a.m. by a dog's peculiar and noisy method of throwing up. *In a minute,* I thought. *In a minute I'll get up and deal with it. In just a minute...*

7:30 a.m.

I open one eye. Luther, ever-hopeful, is standing beside the bed, wagging his tail, ball in his mouth, trying to look cute. Urging me to believe that there is no dog vomit on the rug. I get up, pad to the door in bare feet to let him out. *Should I make a fire, turn on a heater, or pile on clothes and wait for the sun to warm the place?* I pile on clothes and turn on one heater. Compromise is good for the soul.

7:45

I let Luther in, stand in the doorway for a moment and then move on to the deck to greet the morning, the sun, the trees, the pond and the birds. All is well. The mess on the carpet cleans up easily.

8:00

It will be an omelette morning. Yesterday, finally, I found some wild leeks, almost broke an ankle getting them, but they are worth the trouble. A tangy, powerful bite, but gentler than a strong onion. One of them flavours the omelette. I shred a bit of cheese on top, slice a tomato

196

and lay it all on a blue plate with the well-buttered, toasted rosemary bread. Fresh coffee. Life is good.

Luther has expensive kibble, a bit of meat, then waits patiently for dessert—my toast crusts with the tiniest bit of omelette. After all, he did help me find the leeks yesterday.

8:30

Reading, meditating, pondering the vicissitudes of life. Check email for possible world-shaking events which may have transpired since last night. Nothing earth-shaking, but the world is still there, quietly spinning.

9:30

Time to fight with toilet. The pipe to the septic tank is still partially blocked with ice. I attack same with an ugly red plunger, many flushes and kettles of hot water. I abuse the toilet verbally. Toilet just stares wetly at me. Won't release that last chunk of ice.

10:00

Luther is bored. We go for a short walk into the woods. The snow patches are almost gone, pond is almost thawed, trees look expectant. We play throw the ball. *Does he never tire of this game?*

Phone call from friend. Someone has a stray cat, desperate for a home. I respond in negative.

10:30

More coffee. Work on three haikus, fairly new form for me. Sort of like doodling, only more fun.

> Slippery black earth
> Surprised pink geraniums
> Terra-cotta shards.

Sharp regret lifts eyes
Slow wash of pink happiness
Soft dawn of knowing.

Jets trail purity
Clotheslines flung on clean blue sky
Black crows rage dissent.

11:30

Cleaning up kitchen, discover mouse dirt. Throw tantrum. *That
was in the other house!* Like talking to the toilet; complete waste of time.
Luckily, no one hears me except Luther and he doesn't care. Waits for
me to get over it and back to the serious business of ball throwing. *Not
now Luther.* I scour kitchen, bleach is an excellent product (sometimes
I'm very weak-minded and let the cause down badly!) Dead mouse in
trap, dispose of same. He joins his cousin already in the garbage pail.

12:00 noon

Dress for town. Wouldn't hurt to look at the cat.

❉ ❊

9:00 a.m. (the next day)

The pond is almost completely thawed and shimmering like a
Monet painting. A small tortoiseshell cat I have called Gypsy has joined
Luther and me at Walden Three. They are establishing hegemony. Even
though Luther was being very respectful, she hissed at him when he
got too close. Hurt feelings all around.

Vet bills loom, but the "Earth Hour" article will almost pay for
them. Life balances. Eventually.

Green pond shining
Hemlock pointing to heaven
Birdsong swelling heart.

198

finding meaning

This morning, in the second or two before full awareness flooded into consciousness, my mind was jolted by a single thought: *Where is the writing? Where is 'The Book'?*

In the weeks since moving house, I have thought several times of the file folders containing the hard copies of all that I have written in the past few years. Most important are the files containing "The Book" (this one, the one you are holding in your hand). The work that has preoccupied, frustrated, and puzzled me for the past three years. The recent and random thoughts about this work were always wrapped in the secure knowledge that the files were safely tucked away. There were also back-up disks slipped in with them. *So, where are they?*

I knew that during those last chaotic days before moving house, my mind sometimes went elsewhere from where it was supposed to be, somewhere safe to rest and be non-responsible. The memory of what was done or not done in those days either by me or by others, much of it at least, has disappeared into that "resting place". But I know that the files with the writing, I *know* that they were packed away in a large blue laundry basket with a few clothes, toothbrush, soap, a notebook and other essentials that would be needed in that first day or two after the move. But at some time, in spite of my care, those files were taken out of the basket and put in another "safe place". And as often happens, the "safe place" turned out to be anything but safe.

Much of that writing involved this memoir: about Tom and how it was to lose him. Often the writing had felt like collaboration between us so losing the files hurt on many levels. Those files, the hard copies, may or may not be found but I have just bought a "memory stick". Since my computer is almost six years old and aging rapidly, this little gadget that is plugged into it, is my insurance policy to prevent future grief. (The fact that everyone on the planet knew about these "gadgets" before me is more than a little humiliating. The old adage, "Too soon old, too late smart" has applied to me since adolescence.)

Tom said that everything happens for a reason. I'm not sure about that; it falls into the category of puzzling sayings, or sayings that I half-believe until I start thinking seriously about them. I believe that everything that happens has meaning and deciphering that meaning sets one on a spiritual journey that can be pre-occupying for a lifetime, or drive you into the closest psychiatric ward. Or possibly into the nearest church, or to the handiest guru.

But if everything happens for a reason, then the deer I struck while my attention wandered for a split-second while driving on Highway 118 two weeks ago, was either doomed to give up its life to teach me something, or I was doomed to suffer the consequences of hitting the poor creature whose destiny called for her to die at that precise moment. That feels a little preposterous to me. And pretty ego-centric. I believe that as life unfolds, we are able to discover its richness, its many layers, sometimes its comedy, by taking events into our lives with care and attention. That attention allows us to discover one more thread to weave into the tapestry we create simply by being alive and conscious.

Hitting that deer connected me, for a moment, to a world that is normally beyond my ken. A world where predation, famine, deep snow and careless drivers are the stuff of everyday life. A world I entered involuntarily but once entered, I changed the pattern of unfolding in a way I couldn't understand. I could only weep.

A few days later, driving more slowly now than was usual, I passed the spot where I had hit the deer. As my eyes raked both sides of the highway, looking for that sudden awful leap of grace, I slowed even more as I saw, staring out from behind a stand of scrub trees, the unmistakeable, big-eared, big-eyed, face of a young deer. She looked calm; she looked the way a deer usually looks. And she seemed to *see me*, although that may have been my fancy. I drove on, a little unsettled. More than a little moved. Part of my mind started in with the harping that it is so good at. Maybe it was the orphan child of the deer you hit, maybe it was its mother. For a moment the guilt was overwhelming

But I tried to stay with that first sense of seeing that deer as it was seeing me. Nothing more, nothing less. And in some unfathomable way, the universe seemed to click back into place and the rough spot on my soul was gentled away.

Again, I come back to the deer. Just as I am still experiencing the sorting out, the processing, and the search for meaning that began after my encounter with the deer, I am now going through the same digestive process regarding "The Book", my grief, and with Tom himself.

Recently, I have read a strangely powerful book by Cynthia Bourgeault. It is an exploration of the concept that love can survive death; that there is a continuing dialogue and encounter with the loved one, even though one of them is dead. This is not an idea that I would normally pay a lot of attention to; not necessarily because of disbelief but because so many charlatans have become wealthy exploiting the grief of others by means of this same idea. But I have read other works by Bourgeault. She is an intelligent and rather academic theologian, so when I came across a book she wrote a few years ago on how love can not only survive the barrier of death but how both beloveds can continue to grow, continue to do the soul work that was only begun in life, she had my full, if somewhat sceptical attention.

It seems that Tom and I had barely begun our work together. It seems that somehow we lost our place, that sometimes we stood in each other's way, that we blocked the light for each other in some dark and helpless way. And then he died. And everything was so unfinished, so raw and humanly imperfect. Part of my grief fluttered around the idea that nothing was finished, that I lost him too soon.

The stomach-churning sense of loss that I felt when I knew I might have lost the hard copy of my work and the back-up disks woke me to one amazing fact. This work was so important to me not just because of the effort involved in the writing, but because all of a sudden I knew, with simple certainty, that Tom and I had been writing this material together. That the work was not just a tribute to him and to our lives together; not just a phenomenological reflection and meditation on the experience of grief, but rather a profound collaboration of two loving souls, one alive, one dead, who are still loving and laughing together, and who could write a book together. As long as I can keep my eyes on the road, my wits about me and keep on talking to Tom.

"Meaning" is the interpretation we give to events. That interpretation can come from the bulky, often unwieldy package put together by culture, religion and family. But it also arises from the joining of disparate events to create patterns—as though we just *have to* connect the dots to create a constellation so that events have significance. We develop a way not just of making sense of ourselves and our place in the universe, but of noticing synchronicity.

Misplacing my files resulted in a different understanding of the ideas in Bourgeault's book. I understood that Tom and I are joined in a collaboration that is slowly revealing itself, and that I have no logical explanation for.

I still occasionally ask myself "Who's on first?" but I'm not getting stuck there so often. Sometimes it doesn't even matter. I just want to throw balls in the air (or into consciousness) and see what happens.

Hitting a deer and losing (temporarily) my work of three years were profound events for me, full of import. And yet with all the words of the English language at my command, I can't begin to say exactly what that import is. But I know that the struggle to understand, to create meaning, is enough.

exploring grace

Today I sat by the pond listening to frogs murmur to themselves, watching a pair of turtles stretching their necks toward the sun, and thinking of Tom. Of how the five years since his death seemed both a lifetime and a single shuddering moment. And of how he and the gods of real estate had done well in finding this place.

Luther waded knee deep into the water, gazing into its depths, looking for movement. In a moment, Gypsy followed him but only as far as the rocky shore. Having little respect for Luther's hunting skills she found a spot for herself where she was almost hidden by the long grass. She crouched in stillness, watching for movement, for the slightest flicker of life.

Luther kept to the shallows, tail slowly waving, until he spied a frog. Then the tail became a metronome on the verge of a nervous collapse. He lowered his nose to the water, body wiggling in anticipation, thinking he had found a friend. He wanted to play with these elusive creatures.

Or so it seemed. Out of the stillness, more quickly than the leap of a crouching cat, Luther's jaws opened, the great soft paw beat the water, and an inattentive frog will do the backstroke for the rest of its short life.

For a moment, my heart leaped into my mouth and I felt stricken. Luther, my gentle, loving companion had, for a moment, leaped into his own alternate dog reality. And yet, he had pulled back. Maybe it was the taste of raw frog, maybe something else. Instead of pursuing the wounded frog he stepped back and seemed to wear a look of incredulity. Matching mine. His great yellow eyes looked puzzled and unsure. But soon, another frog sprang into view, staring stupidly at Luther. The game began again. Luckily for the frog population his success rate was very low. Gypsy was more adept and only her dislike of water protected the green inhabitants of the pond.

At that moment, for no apparent reason, and with no warning, I was enormously grateful that the weight which had been sitting on my chest for days, the demons of depression who had been nibbling at my spirit, were gone. The wisdom of experience told me that they would be back, but for now, for this day, demons didn't matter. I knew that the blissful sense of this particular now stretching into eternity was enough. Being alive, right here, right now, feeling the sun on my shoulders and a breeze lifting my hair was enough. Nothing more was required.

Hours later when other realities asserted themselves, I remembered the grace of the morning. I kept the memory close until it merged with other memories, other energies. I'm pretty sure Tom was there. Love and laughter and a bit of animal silliness. Where else would he be?

the gates to self-pity

Recently, I have been fighting depression. It was hard to write that sentence even though I know that depression is a very human experience. Churchill wrote about the black dog that followed him all his life. But we live in a world where the darkness of our own shadows seem out-of-place, even shameful. A world dedicated to optimism, affirmations and the healing power of aromatherapy. Not that those things are bad or harmful or unhelpful. But they cannot shed light on grief or the sometimes bone-deep sadness that the world is the way it is.

I have been fighting this bout of depression in the stupidest way possible, by half denying it. Full denial has a certain amount of merit. You can hang out in pyjamas all day and watch soap operas, or you can sit in a bar and drink until someone rolls you home. You can devise various methods of doing yourself in, or you can lie in bed all day sleeping or weeping or staring at the ceiling. You can always find a pill to take the edge off or you can bore your friends by constantly describing how depressed you are. All of these choices have a certain attractive charmlessness and they leave no doubt at all that you are depressed.

But in this state of semi-denial with its impaired sense of reality, the righteous wallowing has been half-hearted. I pluck at the reasons for my distress, reasons that I only half accept.

I occasionally have asked for help with practical matters (moving furniture, putting up shelves) and then felt extreme gratitude tinged with self-pity: if they really knew how pathetic I was they would not regard this as one friend helping another, but as an act of charity. They, after all, are kind people with generous impulses toward the needy.

Perhaps that is the bitter truth I have been so careful to avoid. So, I hide behind humour or heartiness or gratitude. Or I complain in a watery, boring kind of way about the things that really don't matter very much.

The things I can't do (and never actually could do) are piling up in an unseemly way. My theme song seems to be not knowing what to do about things, or how to solve today's problem because yesterday's is still waiting to be solved, or has become unravelled. So I fret and feel that even the things that I might be good at are pretty useless talents right now. It helps and doesn't help that I know so many wonderfully competent women who continually amaze me with their abilities. I have always known women who had excellent home-making skills, the so-called womanly virtues of cooking, sewing, knitting, quilting, canning and cleaning. And I have friends who are amazingly competent at sports, building and fixing things that need fixing and moving things without putting their backs out. They are strong, usually cheerful and take for granted that they can fix a leaky pipe, put up some kitchen shelves and split a cord of wood before lunch. (And I love them anyway.)

Many of the women I know, and I fall down in admiration, can do all or most of these things. They are androgynously and amazingly competent. And I'm not. I do badly at most of the "womanly" qualities, other than cooking where I'm not too bad. But I'm worse in the wood-splitting and shelf building departments.

So here I am, living in the woods, at the age when the government considers me officially old, dealing with a body that doesn't work as well as it used to and not happy that Tom died before I was ready for it. I wish that weren't my realty but it is. If I were to follow the advice in every self-help book out there cluttering up people's book shelves, then this would be about the time when I should try to dredge up all my more stellar qualities. So in no particular order: I'm usually honest, I'm often funny, I'm loyal, usually, to my friends, I'm capable of soul shattering compassion (and not always for myself) and sometimes I can write a good essay or a decent poem. I could say all that, but right now it doesn't seem to matter very much. And that's the whole point, "Mr. Smarty-Pants Self-Help Book Writer".

I know that before you can get out of the cage of depression you must know where the bars are. I feel that I have been flailing around in a kind of murky smog. I know about depression. I've been a therapist for many years and I have been immersed in the journey toward enlightenment long enough to shudder at my loosening grip on self-acceptance and that ego-less nirvana that is so elusive.

I suspect that what I am calling depression is undoubtedly a part, probably a defining part, of being human Regardless of what I know and what I feel; I just need to be there with it, for as long as it takes. Like sitting up with a sick friend. Sometimes just being with oneself is so hard. Long bubble baths and repeating an affirmation twelve thousand times is not going to help much. I came across a sentence the other day in Michael Gellert's *The Way of The Small*: "At a certain point, even wise old women just have to accept who they are and live with it—that's how they become wise."

Bubble baths and affirmations don't work for me. But apparently cleaning out the wood stove, throwing a couple of buckets of ashes down on the ice of the driveway, shovelling the snow away from behind the car so I could turn it around and then, when the shovel broke, kicking the damn stuff out of the way, and finally, de-icing the deck and the steps, does. By then it was time to come in, get a fire going, feed breakfast to Luther and myself and realize that I was as close to exhilaration as I had been in a long while. I may not be Pioneer Lady but I can do stuff. Some stuff. Some of the time. And that must be enough.

I wrote a poem for one of the brave, talented women in my community who is very ill with cancer. The balance shifts and shifts again. And some times the world stops for a moment, it waits for us to catch our breath.

Catching the Camel

In the moment when the world stops spinning,
when my ears fill with stillness,
and my breath stops breathing,

Then in the quiet joy
that catches on my tongue like the delicate taste
of falling snow,
then
my heart knows home.

And the universe,
in its fine generosity,
Pretends it is a camel,
(that grotesquely beautiful creature)
and bends her knee so I can climb upon her back.

In the stillness of that moment,
the camel and my own joyful body
sail into the desert to make the world again.

Playing Poker In The Swamp (one flipper at a time)

Stay in the swamp.
Eat your young.
Gnaw on rancid memories.
Dine on the sour taste of filleted regret
finished
with lashings of malice.

Or.
Put a flipper on solid ground.
Hold your breath. Place a bet; feel the lure
of nothingness.
Wait, as the engine of change
shudders into
the first gear of evolution.

And a watchful frog, hungry for eyelids,
waits her turn
as she ponders cosmology.

acedia

"So, what have you been busy with this summer?"

My friend Lynn, a busy realtor whom I hadn't seen in many weeks, asked this innocent question with an interest that was almost overshadowed by the exhaustion shadowing her face and removing the lilt from her voice. Instantly, I felt guilty. In fact I felt impaled on the end of a sharp stick. I answered clumsily, with generalities, and then quickly changed the subject.

But what I might have said, if honesty had coloured my response rather than mental foot shuffling is: *Bugger all Lynn. I've read some books; some were good, some not so good. Some edifying, some not. I've done some writing. Some not too bad but most just unlovely prose that was squeezed out of the pen like old gummy caulking that got jammed in the gun. I've sat by the pond with Luther and gazed at the frogs practising the nuances of their latest water ballet or staring sullenly at the dog when he tries to interfere. I considered doing a frog head count but have abandoned that idea.*

I could have said to Lynn: *I'm composting—doing a kind of mental and emotional processing that breaks down raw experience and transforms it into understanding. The trouble with that theory is that it ignores the fact that sometimes watching the frogs is just watching the frogs.* But by then I would have lost Lynn in translation.

Maybe I need to be around people who understand the joys and evils of sloth. The other ones, the always usefully busy people, tend to say things like, "Well, I just can't sit around and do nothing." Or

"I need to be doing something, something useful." And obviously watching frogs doesn't cut it.

I remember the time when my life was so filled with parenting and working and socializing that I would yearn for a day when my most onerous duties would be feeding the resident animals and putting out the cushions on the lawn furniture.

And now, most of the time, I am deliriously grateful to have the time and space for what Carl Jung called the task of the second half of life: to discover what it all means, to knit the pieces of one's untidy, disjointed life together and perhaps, find one's God. Or attempt to. When I am full of the writing, of ideas and the joy of living, queries as to what exactly I am doing with my time are irrelevant or meaningless. But if I am trapped by acedia—the alter ego of depression and cousin of sloth, the one who turned out badly and is a disgrace to the family, then questions of any kind become painful.

Acedia is that state when nothing is going well, but worse, when there is no reason to do anything about nothing going well. Kathleen Norris in her book of the same name writes of it as being "a flight from authenticity, from being who you really are". If I am depressed I am despairing of the world and myself. But acedia may or may not involve depression. It just means that whatever I thought was worth doing, isn't. This state of being seems to be a particular enemy of the creative urge. It involves an existential lack of meaning. The world is absurd and so is my life. Lethargy becomes who I am and creative excitement becomes an almost forgotten memory.

My usual way of coping when acedia (the word sounds like a lovely tropical island) wraps its hands around my throat, is to sit by the pond, perhaps counting frogs and praying to the gods of composting. The other choice is to enliven the "gotta-do, gotta-go" persona. Recently I've had less experience with that form of coping. I've also found it works even less effectively than watching frogs, and I don't have the energy for it anymore.

So as I watch the frogs and the way the light falls on the granite outcrops, shifting the patterns of dark and light, I try to accept this lethargic, unhappy aimlessness without allowing it to command all of reality. I wait for the page to turn. And I have faith, most of the time, that the page will turn, that acedia is not a terminal disease. So I will clean the kitchen, go to the dump or take Luther to the park. Or, I might read a sentence in a book (or even write one). Or a friend, maybe a writerly one, will call and we will "speak of walruses and kings" and maybe God, and suddenly, like a tea towel being whisked off the face of the universe, I am awake again and the world seems scrubbed clean.

I think I hear the page beginning to turn, maybe the first line of a poem is bumping against the inside of my head, but it might just be the frogs swallowing flies as they wait for eyelids.

Signs of Life

A blue bathing suit with tired elastic
hangs on a line
disappearing into a pine forest.
A faded blue towel keeps company.

The day bed stretched against the long window,
has a wrinkled cover.
Hieroglyphics left by a human limb or bottom.

On the desk
a flurry of pages,
books in clumsy piles
a Bic pen tossed across a spiral notebook.

A dark blue chair, wide and deep,
a yellow blanket slipping off its back.

A bookshelf overflowing
with stories of turtles, pilgrims and God.

All these things, these necessary things,
remind me of bones,
the necessary bones,
the bones that hold my life.

postscript: about a car

Yesterday I bought a car. More accurately, the bank and I have bought a car.

This car will replace a sporty red Impreza that has never been entirely suitable. Perhaps I am just not a red car person. More likely, the unsuitability has more to do with its lowness to the ground and the depth of its seat. They became somewhat insulting to arthritic knees and backs. So the car will be re-homed with someone more suited to its flirty, low-slung character.

The new one is blue like the colour of a lake after a storm, not quite navy but way beyond royal. And it was that colour that triggered an almost-forgotten memory.

Ten years ago, also in the month of June, Tom and I walked into the local Subaru dealership for the first time. It was the day that my beloved twelve-year-old yellow Jeep had finally given up the ghost. While Tom was driving it home from the dump, the brakes had failed. Luckily, he was almost home and there was no traffic on our quiet country road. The tow truck took it away to the nearest mechanic who happened to be at the Subaru dealership. The verdict was grim. The jeep, like Monty Python's parrot, was dead, deceased, kaput, beyond saving.

And so, needing a second car to get me to work, we decided to buy a big, dark grey, eight year old Oldsmobile 98. But before buying that lovely quite sensible car, we told Charlie that we would take a day to consider our decision.

On our way out we stopped to look at a car that had caught not only my eye, but Tom's. It was a deep blue Outback with classic clean lines. We had already told Charlie, the manager of the dealership, that we couldn't afford a Subaru. We just wanted a reliable second car. Nothing fancy, nothing expensive.

As we stood admiring the Outback, Charlie came up to us and said, "Just get in. You're here anyway. See how it feels."

It was only two years old and had been turned in that very day. I eyed the car. Deep blue with its distinctive grey metal strip that wrapped around the body just below door level. *A very elegant looking car,* I thought, *for a station wagon.* I opened the door, slid into the seat and sank into total comfort. Tom knew how to whisper sweet nothings in my ear. "I can tell by the look on your face, you really like this car. Let's get it!"

For once, sweet nothings didn't move me because I knew the cost of them. So we left the dealership feeling regretful, but I quickly got accustomed to the Oldsmobile that soon became known as Pat's Mafia car.

But yesterday, in the afternoon of a beautiful June day, while looking for a sensible replacement for my lovely but impractical red Impreza, I saw a car, not new, but still quite beautiful. It was a deep blue Outback with its distinctive grey panel. I sat in the driver's seat and sank into a comfort that felt like home. I drove it around the parking lot a time or two, turned to Charlie and said: "How much?"

Turning my head, I thought I heard a chuckle, way off in the distance, from the guy with the deep blue eyes (and a rather mystical relation to money) who wanted me to have this car ten years ago. It just took a while for him to convince me.

acknowledgements

This book would still be sitting on a distant back burner of my mind if it were not for the encouragement and affection of two groups of writers. First, the Algonquin Highlands Writers' Circle—for years of writing, reading and sharing our stories. A circle begun by Brenda Peddigrew seven years ago just as I was beginning to put more energy into writing. Second, my thanks for the feedback and encouragement provided by the *Writers' Croft* and its founder, the amazing Peter Marmorek.

Every second Monday my friend Kathy Purc and I drink tea, talk about books and read each other's current work in progress out loud. This habit has rather destroyed the romantic idea of the solitary writer but it brought another pair of eyes and ears to work that needed attention. I am equally grateful for her insights and her gift for laughter.

Finally, my thanks to the first readers of the manuscript, without whom I might never have pushed the submit button: Judy Breau, Linda McNamara, Brenda Peddigrew, Kathy Purc and John Unrau.